T0149831

Partitioning for Peace

THE INDEPENDENT INSTITUTE is a non-profit, non-partisan, scholarly research and educational organization that sponsors comprehensive studies of the political economy of critical social and economic issues.

The politicization of decision-making in society has too often confined public debate to the narrow reconsideration of existing policies. Given the prevailing influence of partisan interests, little social innovation has occurred. In order to understand the nature of and possible solutions to major public issues, the Independent Institute adheres to the highest standards of independent inquiry, regardless of political or social biases and conventions. The resulting studies are widely distributed as books and other publications, and are publicly debated in numerous conference and media programs. Through this uncommon depth and clarity, the Independent Institute expands the frontiers of our knowledge, redefines the debate over public issues, and fosters new and effective directions for government reform.

THE INDEPENDENT INSTITUTE
100 Swan Way, Oakland, California 94621-1428, U.S.A.
Telephone: 510-632-1366 • Facsimile: 510-568-6040 • Email: info@independent.org • www.independent.org

Partitioning for Peace

An Exit Strategy for Iraq

Ivan Eland

The INDEPENDENT INSTITUTE

Oakland, California

The Independent Institute
100 Swan Way, Oakland, CA 94621-1428
Telephone: 510-632-1366 · Fax: 510-568-6040
Email: info@independent.org
Website: www.independent.org

Cover Design: Christopher Chambers
Cover Image: © Firyal Al-Adhamy, Trees by the Tigris, near Nineveh, 2004, The
Bridgeman Art Library / Getty Images.

Library of Congress Cataloging-in-Publication Data
Eland, Ivan.
    Partitioning for peace : an exit strategy for Iraq / Ivan Eland.
        p. cm.
    Includes bibliographical references and index.
    ISBN-13: 978-1-59813-025-6 (alk. paper)
    ISBN-10: 1-59813-025-0 (alk. paper)
        1. Iraq War, 2003---Peace. 2. Postwar reconstruction--Iraq. 3. Disengagement
(Military science). 4. Peace-building--Iraq. 5. United States--Military relations--Iraq.
6. Iraq--Military relations--United States. 7. Iraq--Politics and government--2003.
8. Internal security--Iraq. 9. United States--Military policy. I. Title.
    DS79.769.E43 2009
    956.7044'31--dc22

                        2008051684

10 9 8 7 6 5 4 3 2 1   09 10 11 12 13

Contents

Introduction

AS OF 2009, the United States has reduced violence in Iraq—albeit to levels considered high before the explosion of violence in 2006 and 2007—mainly by negotiating with or paying off Iraqi groups opposed to the U.S. occupation. The history of violence in multi-ethno-sectarian states, however, indicates that such conflicts usually resurface. The wise adage of former baseball player and manager Yogi Berra likely applies: "It ain't over till it's over."

Despite the U.S. invasion and occupation, the underlying and long-standing ethno-sectarian, tribal, and clan fissures within this artificial country make a unified, democratic Iraq improbable. Even if the fractured Iraqi parliament could pass all of the benchmark laws desired by the U.S. before it ends its occupation, the underlying social fragmentation would most likely render most of them null and void. Experts in democratization believe that a culture of political cooperation is needed before a genuine democratic constitution and laws can be passed and upheld, not vice versa.

The Obama administration intends to begin withdrawing U.S. forces from Iraq. If the goal of a unified, democratic Iraq is a pipe dream, then how can the U.S. withdraw its forces in a dignified way? Fortunately, a silver lining exists in the dark cloud of what has been brutal ethnic and sectarian cleansing. The more homogeneous areas in Iraq—including what were formally mixed cities—now allow for the partition of Iraq into a confederation of autonomous regions or into independent successor states. The United States should threaten to rapidly withdraw all of its military forces in order to put pressure on the Shi'a and Kurds—who dominate the current Iraqi central government—to negotiate such a partition with the Sunnis, who are most reluctant to undertake such a division because there are fewer known oil reserves in their potential autonomous region or independent state (thus leaving them potentially less well off).

Chronic violence and ethnic cleansing have already led to the de facto partitioning of Iraq into the equivalent of armed city-states. Those who oppose partition as a solution need to address the realities on the ground, cope with the unlikelihood that the numerous militias will be disarmed, and come up with a better solution than simply muddling through—which they never do. Such opponents say that Iraqis don't want to subdivide their country, but the actions of many Iraqi groups indicate otherwise. All ethno-sectarian groups currently participating in the Iraqi government claim to be Iraqi nationalists, but they all have starkly different visions about Iraq's future—thus reinforcing the reality of their communal factionalism. In addition, despite the U.S. executive branch's avoidance of partition rhetoric, its policies of arming and training Sunni, Shi'i, and Kurdish groups indicate that the U.S. government also has quietly given up the goal of a unified, democratic Iraq.

Developments in Iraq have shown that the United States cannot really dictate what the Iraqis do about their system of governance. To work, any viable governing arrangement must bubble up from below and not be imposed by a foreign power at gunpoint. The following proposal is just a suggestion to the Iraqis, reflecting their actions already taken on the ground. The Iraqi central government is weak, but probably will need to get weaker. Thus, Iraqis should think about partitioning the country into a confederation of autonomous regions or into independent successor states.

The confederal government proposed here would include all of the autonomous regions, but it would be deliberately kept weaker than the present central government so the various armed groups would not find it necessary to fight for control. Thus, the Iraqi army and national police could be disbanded. Most governance, including the maintenance of security, law enforcement, and judicial functions, would be done at the regional level. The central government would only take the lead in providing diplomatic representation overseas, negotiating trade and financial treaties with foreign nations, and ensuring that free trade and commerce exists among the autonomous regions of the confederation.

The Iraqis themselves would determine regional boundaries and would probably be smart not to use the eighteen arbitrary provisional boundaries now in use. Autonomous regions could be mixed or based on ethno-sectarian or tribal identities. These regions would not have to be limited to three ethno-sectarian regions—one Sunni, one Shi'i, and one Kurd. In a confederation, unlike a federation, various regions could have different forms of government.

An equitable agreement on sharing Iraq's oil would be needed to reduce the possibility of a civil war over the ownership of such resources. Like security, law enforcement, and judicial functions, the central government should have no jurisdiction over resources, thus decreasing the likelihood that armed groups would fight over control of it.

Of course, the partitioning could go even further and create independent successor states. But only the Iraqis should decide the endpoint of the partitioning process.

Ethno-sectarian partitions have gotten a bad name because of violence during partition in other areas—for example, India-Pakistan in 1947, Palestine in 1948, and Ireland in 1921. In all these partitions, however, the problem was not the partition itself—common sense says that separating warring groups should cut down on violence (it has so far in Iraq)—but the fact that they were incomplete and left large minorities on the "wrong" side of the partition line. History shows that large minorities tend to threaten majorities much more than small minorities do, thus leading to more violence. Thus the partition lines must be drawn carefully to avoid stranding large minorities. Since small minorities can exist on the other side of a line, it is a myth that partitions have to be perfect. Also, partition lines should consider resources and cultural or religious shrines.

Among the many lessons that this book gleans from past partitions is that any population movements must be voluntary, can be encouraged with incentives, and must be protected. The most important lesson of past partitions, however, is that all parties must be in agreement with the partition or conflict will result. This is a demanding task, but the current situation of an unratified partition has Iraq on the road to a massive civil war, especially since the United States is training most of the opposing forces. Ratifying and adjusting the existing partition will undoubtedly have problems, but it is the best of many imperfect solutions.

1

The History of a Fractured Land

IRAQ IS AN ARTIFICIAL COUNTRY with only a recent national history. Although Reider Visser, a research fellow at the Norwegian Institute of International Affairs, insists that a divided Iraq is a historical myth, his own data show that Mesopotamia was only united for sixty-eight years of the more than 1,300-year period of Islamic rule in the Middle East between 600 CE and the creation of Iraq by the British after World War I. Although Visser is correct that periodic uprisings during the long era of Islamic rule were not Kurdish or Arabic nationalist in nature (modern nationalism only became a powerful force in the twentieth century as a response to Western colonialism in non-Western areas that began in the latter half of the nineteenth century), he does admit that, during that extended period, sporadic revolts in Kurdish areas and sectarian Shi'i–Sunni conflict arose.[1] Almost all of Iraq's tribal and ethno-sectarian groups place loyalty to their group above allegiance to the nation. Without an iron-fisted ruler there is little chance that Iraq will remain unified in the long term.

Thus, Iraq is likely to be partitioned (into autonomous regions or independent states) one way or another. It can be partitioned by full-blown civil war or it can be partitioned by a peacefully negotiated settlement. In fact, to some extent, Iraq is already partitioned into autonomous areas, with local forces providing security and governance. This unratified partition is dangerous. It is in the interest of the United States to help facilitate a peacefully negotiated partition, to be ratified by all of Iraq's heterogeneous groups, and then rapidly withdraw its military forces from that land.

The Ottoman Empire and Before

Iraq has only been a country since the victorious British, after World War I, artificially drew lines on a map and combined three disjointed former provinces of the defeated Ottoman Empire—Mosul, Baghdad, and Basra—into the new League of Nations–mandated British protectorate of Mesopotamia (the name *Iraq* evolved later). And as Edwin Black, the author of a history of Iraq, implies, the lack of unity among these provinces preceded even the Ottoman Turks' conquest of Mesopotamia during the Safavid Persian Empire in 1534.

> For centuries ahead, Mesopotamia would be a mere grouping of outpost provinces, once again ruled from afar by a foreign people—this time the Ottomans. As before, devoid of national identity or cohesion, Mesopotamian society distilled down to its basic units—the clan and the tribe against everyone and anyone.[2]

The violent conflict between the Sunni and Shi'i versions of Islam—which are based on different views of who should have succeeded Mohammed as head of the faith and which can trace their deep roots back to the religion's youth in the 600s CE—raised its ugly head in Mesopotamia. According to Gareth Stansfield, associate professor of Middle East politics at the University of Exeter, this original schism of Islam into Sunni and Shi'i factions was a defining moment in Iraq's history. Yet he also notes correctly that the modern-day Shi'i–Sunni cleavages are not based on sectarian differences alone; they also derive from Sunni political and economic dominance over the Shi'a during the Ottoman Empire and in every Iraqi government up until the U.S. deposed Saddam Hussein, and from the more religious nature of the Shi'i community compared to that of the Sunnis (today there are no secular Shi'i political parties).[3]

In the early 1500s, Ismail I, the shah of Safavid Persia, demanded that the predominant Sunni sect in that nation convert to Shi'ism. Ismail then forced Sunnis in Mesopotamia—all three regions of which the

Persians conquered to safeguard the holiest Shi'i religious shrines in Najaf—into a similar conversion. The Sunni Ottoman Turks frowned on this development and invaded Mesopotamia, displaced the Safavid Persians, and ruled the three Mesopotamian regions from around 1535 until the British took over from the defeated Ottoman Empire after World War I.

Middle Eastern specialist Charles Tripp, who wrote a history of Iraq, concurs with Edwin Black that the Ottoman provinces of what is now Iraq had no national identity before the British created the country not all that long ago (in terms of ethno-sectarian heritage):

> It would be fanciful to assume that in the years leading up to the British occupation of Mesopotamia, the future state of Iraq was somehow prefigured in the common experiences of these provinces. In many respects, the central political relationship with the Ottoman state was broadly similar to that of the other Arab provinces. . . . From the perspective of the government in Istanbul, the three Mesopotamian provinces were neither treated administratively as a unit, nor accorded any form of collective representation that set them apart from other regions of the empire.[4]

Even Peter Sluglett—a professor of Arab Middle East history at the University of Utah who believes that most of Iraq's current ethno-sectarian tensions are rooted not in long-term grievances, but rather in Saddam's setting the groups against each other and the U.S. occupation exacerbating such recently induced tensions—admits that the Sunni elite argued in the early 1920s "that however faintly Iraq might resemble an independent Arab state, it was at least 'more Arab' in its administration and certainly more of a coherent entity than the three provinces had been under Ottoman rule."[5]

The Ottoman Empire grew very weak centuries before it collapsed after losing the Great War. In fact, the empire was so weak that it relied on local rulers in fragmented Mesopotamia. For example, from 1733 until the early 1800s, local rulers governed the province of Baghdad without interference from Istanbul, the Ottoman capital, and refused to send more than token tribute to the Ottomans. By the early 1800s, the provinces of Mesopotamia, although nominally still under Ottoman rule, were so autonomous that they were subject to a struggle for power raging between the pasha of Baghdad, the Persians, the British, the Indians, and occasionally the fanatical Wahhabi religious armies from Arabia. During the later Ottoman era, the Kurds wanted to be independent. The Shi'a in southern Mesopotamia simply ignored the Sunni Ottoman institutions.

In the 1820s, a new sultan, Mahmud II (Mahmud the Reformer), came to power in the Ottoman Empire. He wanted to bring Western ideas into the decaying empire and also to reconquer the autonomous provinces of Mesopotamia. Daoud Pasha, the ruler of Baghdad, was amassing wealth and power comparable to the sultan's, yet he refused to send taxes and tribute to the sultan, and he failed to defend Karbala (in modern-day southern Iraq) from Wahhabi armies. The sultan demanded a huge tribute from Daoud, and Daoud declined to provide it. In 1831, the sultan's armies took Baghdad and deposed Daoud. Mahmud next turned to Karbala—an independent Shi'i city run by Persians and criminal gangs—to reassert Ottoman control, but he had difficulty and died before he could subdue it. In 1843, desiring to "Turkify" the Shi'i city, the Sunni Ottomans, under a new sultan, penetrated the city's wall, looted the city, raped the women, and slaughtered men, women, and children. In all, 15 percent of the city's population was brutally massacred.[6] The Ottomans also reconquered the cities of Basra and Mosul, but this victory did not result in control of the tribes in the countryside. Those pieces of Mesopotamia were returned to the Ottomans but were hardly a unified region. In fact, piecemeal efforts by the Ottomans to strengthen and standardize the rule of their empire only led to more political and social fragmentation in Mesopotamia.[7]

In sum, the Ottomans (with a fairly small administrative bureaucracy in absolute numbers), and later the British colonial overlords, would rule Mesopotamia by relying on decentralized methods—that is, governing through regional leaders or tribal chiefs.[8] Istanbul had little control over the three provinces, and the governors of the provinces had little control over the tribes within them. Because of their weakness, the Ottomans developed a "divide and conquer" strategy. The Ottomans encouraged rivalry between tribes, ethnic and sectarian groups, and social classes, which led to the retention of strong communal groups throughout the Mesopotamian area.[9]

World War I

Even before the major battles in Europe during World War I, the British had invaded Persia and Mesopotamia. They wanted to safeguard the oil refinery at Abadan, Persia, which the British government-controlled Anglo-Persian Oil Company (later British Petroleum) had recently built. The British also feared that the upcoming war would impede movement of oil from this refinery through the Persian Gulf because the port of Basra was in Mesopotamia, which the enemy Ottomans controlled. Although no oil drilling concessions had yet been granted in Mesopotamia, the British wanted this port to ensure that this critical Persian oil flowed to the British navy for the war effort.

After the Ottoman Turks had opted to side with Germany in the war, but before Britain declared war on the Ottoman Empire, the order went out to colonial Indian naval forces poised near Abadan to make war against the Turks. One day after the British declaration against the Turks, Indian forces captured the Anglo-Persian refinery, and British and Indian forces later occupied Basra. From Basra, their most important objective, the British decided to move north to conquer more of Mesopotamia. But some Arabs and Kurds had joined the Ottoman jihad against the British, and it took the British a year and a half and tens of thousands of lives just to make the short trip to Baghdad.

The British had promised the Arabs post–World War I independence if they helped the British and rebelled against their Ottoman overlords. But the British excepted Basra, Baghdad, and Mosul from the offer of independence; they wanted to occupy these areas because of their likely future role in the oil business. In early 1916, while the war still raged, however, the British, French, and Russians negotiated the secret Sykes-Picot Agreement to carve up the Middle East. The French wanted Mosul because, unlike the British, they had no Middle Eastern oil fields. The British kept the Ottoman provinces of Basra and Baghdad, but pledged to give up Mosul to the French in order to assure safe passage of oil and commerce from southern Mesopotamia, Persia, and the Persian Gulf through Syrian ports (the French controlled Syria at that time) to the Mediterranean Sea. Thus oil would move south to Basra and the Persian Gulf and west through Syria and Palestine to the Mediterranean. No one ever asked the Arabs their opinion, and the separate principalities of Syria, Mosul (both French), Baghdad, and Basra (both British) were designed to keep the Arabs divided and weak against their colonial masters.[10] Thus, at this point, the colonial powers were not thinking in terms of uniting the three provinces that are now called Iraq.

But the French were never to get Mosul. The British knew that valuable oil deposits lay underneath the soil there and began scheming to retain that Ottoman province just after signing the Sykes-Picot Agreement with the French. The British wanted to control the oil deposits in Persia and Mesopotamia for industrialization and for fuel in their warships to police their still growing, but decaying, empire.

Unlike the French, the British had enough military forces in what is now Iraq to make possession of Mosul nine-tenths of the law. When the Ottoman Empire surrendered in October 1918, British forces stopped forty miles south of Mosul. The armistice with the Ottomans called for the surrender of all Ottoman military bases in "Syria and Mesopotamia." The British took advantage of the fact that the term "Mesopotamia" was not in official use in the Ottoman Empire. The British wanted Mosul, but the Ottoman governor protested that Mosul was not in Mesopotamia. Declaring them in violation of the cease-fire, the British demanded that the Turks evacuate Mosul, and then the British marched into the city.

According to Edwin Black, "An uneasy new national outline had been cobbled together that was mainly Kurdish in the north, Sunni in the midsection, and Shiite in the south." British civil administrator Arnold Wilson, essentially the creator of Iraq, noted that "we had established de facto, the principle that the Mosul vilayet [province] is part of Iraq" and so "laid the foundation stone of the future State of Iraq."[11] Although British forces occupied Mosul, the British Foreign Office sent a message to Wilson ordering him to govern Basra and Baghdad separately and to maintain only a defensive military position in Mosul. In contravention of these orders, Wilson, on his own, decided to administer all three provinces together from Baghdad—thus creating Iraq. The situation on the ground essentially rendered the Sykes-Picot Agreement null and void. The French eventually gave up their territorial claim on Mosul in exchange for a substantial percentage of Mosul's oil. The British got 55 percent ownership of Mesopotamia's oil, the French received 25 percent, and the local inhabitants 20 percent. Later, by the late 1920s, the Americans demanded and got a percentage of Iraqi (and Middle Eastern) oil, and the ownership share for local inhabitants was eliminated in exchange for a share of the royalties.[12]

According to Gareth Stansfield, the European concept of a "melting pot" of peoples brought together in a sovereign territory with a cohesive national identity is foreign to the Middle East and Iraq. In contrast, most modern Middle Eastern states are fragments of empires containing rival groups. He further notes that at the time the British created it,

> Iraq was a powder keg of considerable dimensions, and was certainly not a logical construct in a domestic sense. Indeed, the political and economic lives of the communities of the Ottoman *vilayets* [provinces] remained loosely focused upon their major towns of Mosul, Baghdad and Basra, with a strong rural-urban divide being evident, and each of these towns existing within quite separate geo-economic and political spheres with Mosul being linked with Anatolia and acting as a bridge with Iran, Baghdad looking westwards towards the Arab lands and Basra having a notably "Gulf-centric" identity. It is clear that the boundaries of Iraq were drawn not by "some irreducible essence of Iraqi history." Instead, Iraq was cre-

ated because of the logics of colonial and imperial power. Far from emerging from the natural interaction of the communities of the region, the Iraqi state was imposed from afar.[13]

Charles Tripp best sums up Britain's creation of the artificial, faction-ridden country of Iraq out of whole cloth:

> The British invasion and occupation of the three Ottoman provinces of Basra, Baghdad and Mosul and their subsequent consolidation into the new state of Iraq under a League of Nations Mandate administered by Great Britain radically changed the political worlds of the inhabitants of these territories. The history of Iraq begins here, not simply as the history of the state's formal institutions, but as the histories of all those who found themselves drawn into the new regime of power. It demanded new forms of identity. . . . Of the three million or so inhabitants of Iraq at the beginning of the Mandate, more than half were Shi'i and roughly 20 percent were Kurdish, with another 8 percent or so composed of the Jewish, Christian, Yazidi, Sabaean, and Turkmen minorities. Yet the government ministers, the senior state officials and the officer corps of the armed forces were drawn almost exclusively from the Sunni Arabs, who constituted less than 20 percent of the population. Given their minority position, in economic and sectarian terms, as well as their authoritarian inclinations, this was not a promising basis for the national integration that was in theory intended to accompany the construction of the modern state.[14]

In short, although Iraqi nationalism was practically nonexistent in Mesopotamia after World War I, these three provinces of Mesopotamia—Kurdish, Shi'i, and Sunni—increasingly were labeled "Iraq."

Although Stansfield seems to admit that Iraq was an artificial state when the British created it, he reports the argument that Iraq has now lasted almost one hundred years and has developed its own momentum and nationalism among the population to support it.[15] This supposed momentum toward integration, however, went in reverse after the U.S. invaded the country. This paper will show, by studying other countries' partitions, that ethno-sectarian forces, often powerful, can bubble up and defeat nationalism in multi-ethno-sectarian states decades, and even centuries, later.

Inter-War Years

After World War I, the European victors adopted subtler and more "politically correct" forms of colonialism to replace the independence for Arabs that was promised to get them to fight their Ottoman overlords during the war. With little regard for what native peoples wanted, the great powers created League of Nations–approved "mandates" for nations targeted for eventual self-determination, but which weren't yet prepared to stand on their own (in the opinion of the great powers).[16] France got Syria and Lebanon, and Britain got Palestine, Jordan, and Mesopotamia.

The U.S. government—a government that was supposed to be anti-colonial and promoting Woodrow Wilson's doctrine of self-determination for foreign peoples—secretly believed that foreign overlords would be needed to forge unified nations out of the tribal peoples of Syria and Mesopotamia.[17] Similarly, as Black noted, to tame Mesopotamia the British had to do more than defeat the Ottomans. They had to deal with "a fractious jumble of tribal rivalries and alliances." Black further notes that "the alienation Mesopotamian Shi'i felt for the Sunni majority [in the larger Islamic world] never subsided. Hence, the ancient Shi'a-Sunni rivalries and ingrained disregard for infidels held fast."[18]

Also, from the time of the British mandate, periodic Kurdish revolts have erupted. Kurdish nationalism per se didn't manifest itself until other nationalisms arose in the twentieth century as a reaction to European colonialism. But Kurdish anger has centered on the creation of the Iraqi state itself, which in part denied them their own state, which was promised to them in an international treaty after World War I.[19] Moreover, the persistence and strengthening of the Kurdish identity under-mines even the idea of an Iraqi nationalism.

Even Peter Sluglett, who believes Saddam is mainly responsible for Iraq's current ethno-sectarian tensions, admits:

> The notion that pan-Arabism had broad appeal in interwar Iraq has become part of the "standard account" of Iraqi history, but it is at least questionable that the doctrine was quite as widely ac-cepted as has been claimed. The ethnic and sectarian composition of Iraq makes it difficult to imagine that an essentially Sunni Arab vision of the Arabic-Islamic world would have been the "doctrine of choice" of a population whose composition was more than half Shi'i and at least one-fifth Kurdish.[20]

The heavy-handed British occupation, however, was very unpopular with the natives and resulted in a state of near war with the occupiers. Arnold Wilson imported Indian law, officials, and laborers into Iraq; took land, property, and water for the British military and administra-tion; conscripted local inhabitants away from their jobs to do mandatory jobs for the occupiers at low pay; and heavily controlled the movement of individuals and scarce food, thus letting tribes unfriendly to the Brit-ish starve. When the new British commander of the Shi'i city of Najaf decided to retaliate in the wake of citizen unrest, he was assassinated. Wilson then ordered all food and water to Najaf cut off until the assas-sins were surrendered and the city paid a fine; he also refused to evacuate the women and children. Najaf, its water almost out after weeks of siege, eventually surrendered the killers.

In most Arabic regions, the inhabitants were unhappy about getting mandates instead of promised independence after the war. But resis-tance to the British was greatest in Iraq. As in the U.S. occupation of Iraq today and the U.S. and Soviet Union occupations of Afghanistan, the Russians in Chechnya, the Israelis in Palestine, and the U.S. in Leb-anon in the 1980s, a major grievance causing violence is the non-Muslim occupation of Muslim land.

In 1919 and 1920, the year the mandate was assigned to Britain, Iraq erupted in revolt. The uprisings were mainly among the Kurds and Shi'i tribes, with little coordination between them, and opposition to the rebellion from the Sunni elite in Baghdad. Although the 1920 revolt is regarded as the beginning of Iraqi nationalism, resistance was already fragmented among various groups.

The British occupiers—having too few forces to fight the rebels on the ground (29,500 mostly Indian soldiers versus 160,000 fighters in Baghdad and Basra and 481,000 Kurds from Mosul) and facing insurgents that were spread out and hiding in the mountains in the Mosul area—indiscriminately bombed civilian areas. Such bombing by Air Marshal Chief Arthur "Bomber" Harris—who later, in World War II, carried out the brutal firebombing of Germany—was designed to erode the morale of the Iraqi population to resist. The British also responded to insurgent attacks by burning villages and crops. Today, such deliberate attacks on civilians would be called "terrorism" or "war crimes."

In addition to brutal tactics, the British decided to try to cow the religious centers of the rebellion. They blockaded the holy city of Karbala and interdicted the canals to cut off water. In Najaf, they threatened to bomb the city unless it submitted. Both cities threw in the towel. The subjugation of the two holy sites and the reduction of outside funding for the insurrection, which dried up the supply of ammunition for the rebels, took the fire out of the insurrection. In November 1920, the British quickly established a new provisional government with an elected assembly and a process to write a constitution. This action also helped take the energy out of the insurgency. In the summer of 1921, the British brought in a new ruler, whom the French had kicked out of Syria in 1920—Hashemite King Faisal—and the new nation of Iraq was created. Because the Shi'a were prominent in the revolt, the British selected ex-Ottoman Sunnis to populate the new Iraqi government and army.[21]

According to Stansfield, "For [King] Faisal, political survival meant building consensus and unity within Iraq, effectively bringing together diverse peoples with little history of political community into a national project." He further wrote, "With hindsight the 1920 revolt had forced the British to enact a solution which simply did not serve to forge the various segments of Iraqi society into an organic nation, but instead created an entity that would need to be maintained by force for nearly 40 years."[22] In fact, it should be argued that force has been required to hold Iraq together until the present. Stansfield notes that from the 1920s on, "in the north, Kurdish tribes remained in a state of perpetual revolt, and political authority in the south and west of the country remained in the hands of prominent tribes. Perhaps most worrying was the ongoing hostility of the Shi'i population towards the newly appointed king."[23]

The British suppressed the 1920 revolt successfully, but no rejoicing occurred in Britain. The British press and public were glum over the costs in lives, taxpayer dollars, and future debt, which had accumulated quelling the Iraqi rebellion of 1920. The lives of five hundred British and Indian soldiers had been lost. The Iraqis were not rejoicing either. Six thousand Iraqis had been killed. Their country had been torched in many places, and the king was a figurehead who was still under the British mandate. The Sunni king wanted gradual independence from British control and integration of the diverse communities of Iraq into a unified country. According to Tripp, he made progress on the first, but was foiled on the second because of the "flawed nature of the enterprise"—that is, he had little support among the Kurds and Shi'a.[24] Although the League of Nations mandated British "protection" until the supposedly fragile country could stand on its own, the only things being protected by the British military were British economic interests from some uncooperative Iraqis.

In 1922, uncertainty existed about whether Mosul would remain in Iraq and where its boundaries were. Britain had questionably grabbed the province in violation of the cease-fire between the Ottoman Turks and the British after World War I had ended. The reconstituted smaller state of Turkey now wanted the oil-rich province back, but the British said no. Cleverly, Turkey stood behind U.S. President Woodrow Wilson's concept of self-determination and demanded a referendum by the

Kurds and Arabs of the Mosul province about whether they wanted to stay in the British mandate or be reincorporated into Turkey. Instead of a referendum, the League of Nations, which was dominated by the powers allied with Britain during World War I, cited Turkey's human rights issues and Kurdish noises about independence (still heard strongly today) as it declared that Mosul would remain in the British mandate of Iraq. The autonomy-seeking Kurds, with the help of the Turks, revolted in 1923. The British then pummeled the Kurdish city of Sulaimaniyya with air power and subsequently occupied it with ground forces. The Iraqi government, dominated by the Sunni minority, supported the British suppression because if the province of Mosul had separated, the restive Shi'a would have had an even larger majority in the rump state, which would have been even more difficult to control. The Kurds continued guerrilla warfare against the British and the Iraqi government until the early 1930s and sporadically thereafter.

In 1930, by signing the Anglo-Iraqi Treaty, Britain allowed oil-rich Iraq to become a quasi-independent country in exchange for retention of two air bases, more military basing, and transit rights in case of a conflict. In 1932, the League of Nations removed the mandate and admitted Iraq as a member.[25] According to Tripp,

> The period of the Mandate had been a defining period in many ways. It had not only laid the institutional foundations of the Iraqi state and demarcated its territorial boundaries, but had also made the state the principal arena for the multiple struggles that were to constitute a distinctively Iraqi politics. On one level, it had unmistakably made of Iraq a British imperial project, corresponding in its shape and in its constitution to ideas current in Great Britain about the proper organization of power.[26]

In the 1930s, the tradition began of Iraqi authoritarians using armed forces to control the heterogeneous and fractious country. This is again best summarized by Charles Tripp:

The educational system became increasingly militarised as politicians tried to inculcate the virtues of discipline and obedience in the hope of creating an ordered, submissive society out of Iraq's fractious population. . . . By introducing military training to schools and teachers' training colleges in 1935–6 . . . state officials were trying to ensure disciplined acceptance of the status quo in the name of some variety of nationalism. Yet the complex of relationships and power that constituted the status quo was far removed from any such national, collective ideal. It was founded instead on economic privilege, status hierarchies, and multiple forms of discrimination—tribal, familial, sectarian, and ethnic—that vitiated any practical form of either Iraqi or Arab nationalism.[27]

World War II

In 1941, the British were afraid that France's mandates of Syria and Lebanon—which were run, after the fall of France to the Nazis in 1940, by a collaborationist Vichy French government—would allow the Nazis to occupy those countries and use them as a base to invade the oil fields in Iraq, which were viewed as vital to the war effort of both sides. From there, the British were afraid the Nazis would push farther east, skirting Russia. In the spring of 1941, there was a pro-axis uprising in Iraq.[28] Britain ordered that Abd al-Ilah, Iraq's pro-British regent (ruling Iraq for the young King Faisal II), dump Prime Minister Rashid Ali al-Kailani to foil the aspirations of the Arab nationalist, anti-British, and thus pro-German Iraqi Golden Square—a group of four power brokers in the Iraqi army. But the Golden Square learned of the plans, surrounded the palace, and attempted to arrest the regent. The regent escaped, but the Golden Square appointed a new pro-German regent. The new Iraqi government was pro-German, hating the British Empire, which still had bases and much influence in Iraq long after that nation had become "independent" in the early 1930s.

German troops were readying themselves to enter Vichy-run Syria and, with the help of a pro-German government in Iraq, occupy the Iraqi oil fields. The British then decided that they had better destroy Iraq's oil facilities to prevent the Nazis from getting them. But Britain retained only a skeleton military presence in Iraq at that time, and the pro-German Iraqi government moved troops to guard such facilities. As Iraqi troops approached the large British air base at Habbaniya, west of Baghdad between Fallujah and Ramadi, the British began firing. The base was home to a British military flight school, and the students attacked the Iraqi vehicles at a choke point in a road and turned them into junk. Germans then bombed the Habbaniya base from a base in Vichy-run Syria and one they had set up in Mosul.

Now that Nazis had air power in Iraq, it was a threat to the Suez Canal and the large British oil refinery in Abadan, Persia. Just as the British were readying to destroy Iraqi oil pipelines and refineries, they got the upper hand in the battle for Habbaniya. They then organized a British-led Arab legion that defeated exhausted Iraqi ground forces, weathered German air attacks, and captured Baghdad. Unlike 1923, when the Shi'a and Kurds opposed the British-backed, Sunni-dominated Iraqi government in its effort to overrun Kurdistan, this time the Shi'a and Kurds were not enthusiastic about helping the Sunni-dominated Golden Square against the British. In quarrelsome Iraq, the downtrodden Kurds and Shi'a seem to have been more consistent in their opposition to the Sunnis than to British colonial power.

Although German bomber crews evacuated from Mosul back to Germany, a new German move into Vichy Syria and Lebanon was afoot. British, Australian, and Free French forces, aided by Jewish commandos that included future Israeli leaders Moshe Dayan and Yitzhak Rabin, attacked Vichy forces in Syria and Lebanon from Iraq, Palestine, and the sea and defeated them. The offensive secured airfields and oil facilities and denied the Nazis a base from which to commandeer Iraqi oil. In June 1941, Hitler had to invade Russia without possessing Iraqi oil.[29]

Post–World War II

Journalist Edwin Black best summed up Iraq in the post–World War II era as a series of coups, insurrections in the north (by the Kurds) and south (by the Shi'a), religious strife between the Sunnis and Shi'a, and a resentment of foreign interference.[30] All of these historical forces in Iraq have played a role in shaping the current argumentative milieu after an invasion by a foreign occupier (the United States) smashed the brutal dictatorial rule that had traditionally held the country together—from local rulers during the Ottoman Empire, through British colonial rule, to post-British Iraqi strongmen, including Saddam Hussein.

Resentment of foreign exploitation of its oil hampered Iraqi petroleum production compared to its oil-rich neighbors. After Iran nationalized foreign petroleum interests in 1951 and Saudi Arabia negotiated a fifty-fifty split of oil profits, Iraqis wanted, and in 1952 also received, such a division. During the Cold War, this Iraqi resentment was exacerbated by Britain's desire to maintain a robust military presence in Iraq to guard Western oil interests. In 1955, to create a barrier to potential Soviet expansion in the Near East, the British—along with Iraq, Iran, Turkey, and Pakistan—created the Baghdad Pact alliance. Some in the Iraqi military regarded this alliance as merely one more capitulation to British and Western oil interests.

Egyptian leader Gamal Abdel Nasser, the pan-Arab nationalist and anti-Western leader who sidled up to the Soviet Union to offset Western influence in the Middle East, captured and used such nationalist resentments. In 1958, Nasser's Egypt had formed a union with faraway Syria in the United Arab Republic (UAR). To compete with this alliance for pan-Arab primacy, the Iraqi and Jordanian Hashemite monarchies, which conservatively desired to rein in Nasser's push for rapid social and political revolution, joined together in the Arab Union. But Nasser's anti-Western and pan-Arab nationalist posture struck a chord with the Iraqi people and elements of Iraq's armed forces. A Nasser-inspired coup by the Iraqi military in July 1958 overthrew and killed the Iraqi Hashemite King Faisal II and also executed long-influential Iraqi Prime Minister Nuri al-Sa'id.

Stansfield argues that from 1958 on, a secular and non-communal nationalism emerged in Iraq, which, he admits, was eventually undermined by Saddam's later wars and divisive repression of ethno-sectarian groups, resultant U.N. sanctions during the 1990s, ill-advised actions during the U.S. occupation, and rise of the Islamist movement—all of which sent economic development and the urban middle class packing along with the Iraqi nationalism built upon these pillars. Stansfield acknowledges, however, that communalism was prevalent in Mesopotamian society before the British created Iraq.[31]

A more probable interpretation is that the secular and non-communal nationalism was a paper-thin covering for the longer-lasting divisive reality underneath. Furthermore, even after the 1958 coup, the Sunni ruling group's pan-Arab nationalism, which attempted to tie the Sunni regimes of the Middle East together, scared the Kurds and Arab Shi'a, who were a large majority in Iraq but a small minority in the wider Middle East.

Abd al-Karim Qasim, the new autocrat and prime minister, recognized Nasser's UAR but was ostensibly an Iraq-first socialist instead of a pan-Arab nationalist. Like the Hashemite monarch before him and Iraqi governments after him, Qasim would claim to be an Iraqi nationalist but would rule by a web of patronage links based on clan, tribe, and ethno-sectarian identities (periodic rhetoric to the contrary, very few Iraqi rulers have tried to promote an Iraqi identity and unify these disparate groups under it).

The Syrian military mobilized on Jordan's border, and the UAR warned Lebanon's leaders they were next in line. Because Jordan and Lebanon—the latter roiled by internal conflict—urgently sent out an SOS, the British sent airborne troops to Jordan and the Americans sent Marines to Lebanon.[32] Although Nasserite forces had Egypt and Syria, had just turned Iraq, and were threatening Jordan and Lebanon, Jordan and Lebanon were not strategic to the United States (they didn't have any oil); thus, the motives for this Eisenhower intervention in Lebanon were questionable.

The Kurds took advantage of the coup in Baghdad and ratcheted up their rebellion in Mosul province in the north. Qasim ruthlessly repressed the Kurds and consolidated his power in Baghdad. The draconian repression of the Kurds lasted until 1962. From the 1958 coup onward, periodic Kurdish rebellions became better organized and received more assistance from outside powers that were unfriendly to Iraq.

Qasim, in the meantime, had withdrawn Iraq from the Baghdad Pact and began to rely on the Soviet Union for arms and foreign assistance. In 1960, in response to communist USSR's slashing oil prices to recapture market share and normally competition-averse Western oil oligopolies following suit, Qasim organized the Organization of Petroleum Exporting Countries (OPEC) in an attempt to keep prices artificially elevated.[33]

In the winter of 1962–1963, the Kurdistan Democratic Party decided the only way to resolve their violent dispute with the Iraqi government was to overthrow Qasim. It offered a cease-fire in the ongoing rebellion if he were ousted.[34] In February 1963, in another coup, disgruntled military officers, who were sympathetic to pan-Arab Baathism and Nasser's Arab nationalism, killed Qasim, an Iraq-first socialist. The cease-fire did not last long, however, as the Kurds resumed their perennial guerrilla rebellion for regional autonomy. In the 1960s, they moved from being hit-and-run guerrillas to holding a large amount of Iraqi territory and setting up governance in it.

Like Nasser in Egypt and their fellow Baathists in Syria, the Iraqi Baathists were socialists but gave pan-Arab nationalism an even higher priority. That is, they believed that there was a single Arab nation that had the right to a unified Arab state.[35] Thus they were more like the national socialists of Germany or the fascists of Italy than the more internationally oriented communists. But the Arif family, at least initially also pan-Arab socialists, quickly threw the Baathists out of power in late 1963 and ruled by the familiar networks of kinship, tribal links, and patronage.[36]

In 1968, yet another putsch brought the Baathists back into power. Ahmad Hassan al-Bakr, the new Baathist ruler, was one more ruthless Iraqi strongman. The regime nationalized Western petroleum interests, relied more on the Soviet Union to help with oil exploration, and thus set itself up to benefit from the spike in world oil prices after the 1973 oil embargo and Middle East war—giving the regime far more patronage to hand out compared with prior Iraqi governments. Later Baathist Iraq, to a certain extent, patched up its relations with the West.[37] Also, as under Qasim, the Sunni ruling elite under al-Bakr committed horrors against the Kurds. But the Kurds gained their first breath of autonomy in Iraq from 1970 to 1974.

In 1975, the U.S. supported the shah of Iran against Iraq, which had Soviet military advisors, in a border dispute. Secretary of State Henry Kissinger encouraged another Kurdish rebellion against Iraq. After Iraq and Iran settled the border dispute in Iran's favor, the Iraqi army was freed up to smash the revolt. The Kurdish rebellion collapsed without continued Iranian assistance. When the Kurds appealed to Kissinger for support, he coldly said, "Covert action should not be confused with missionary work."[38] Without Iranian and U.S. support, the uprising was doomed. Sadly, this was not to be the last time that the Kurds would follow U.S. prodding to revolt against the Iraqi government, only to see U.S. support evaporate and their uprising brutally crushed by an Iraqi strongman.

The Sunni Baathist leadership in Iraq became alarmed that exiled Iranian Shi'i Grand Ayatollah Ruhollah Khomeini's fundamentalist verbal attacks on the shah of Iran from the Iraqi holy city of Najaf were stirring up Iraqi Shi'a, and they expelled him in October 1978. Khomeini then went to Paris, organized a revolution in Iran from exile, and triumphantly returned to Iran and took power in February 1979. The Iranian revolution and the Iraqi governmental repression of its Shi'i populations then motivated Iraqi Shi'i organizations to campaign more ardently against the Baathist government. Like all prior Arab and Iraqi nationalist governments in Iraq, the Sunni Baathists traditionally were leery of the Iraqi Shi'a, fearing that their sectarian brothers and sisters in Iran—Iraq's longtime archenemy—would sway the Shi'a. Fearing rising Shi'i power in Iraq, Baathist al-Bakr and Saddam Hussein, his kinsman and chief enforcer, arrested and expelled thousands of Shi'a, including top Shi'i clerics.

In mid-July 1979, al-Bakr resigned for "health reasons," and Saddam, taking advantage of the crisis, replaced him as ruler of Iraq and then purged the Baath Party.[39] Although not officially the top man prior to this switch, Saddam had dominated the Baathist regime since 1976 and ruled through the usual ethno-sectarian, tribal, and clan patronage networks. Considering this method of rule, Middle East specialist Charles Tripp reaches an ominous conclusion for a post-Saddam Iraq:

> Another important element that was reinforced during the years of Saddam Hussain's rule were the societal networks of kinship and patronage. . . . So widespread has it become as a practice, even amongst those most vehemently opposed to the previous regime, that it raises the question of whether such networks can be truly integrated into a national state of accountable institutions. By their very ability to get things done, organizing power and channeling resources, these forms of political activity may once again delay or even prevent the emergence of such a state.[40]

Saddam was just another in a long line of iron-fisted rulers who kept the three disparate and fractious provinces of the former Ottoman Empire artificially together in one country. According to Tripp, Saddam created the myth of an Iraqi identity.[41] Many observers today, who hold out the hope that the unity of Iraq can be preserved even in the wake of the years post Saddam ethno-sectarian tension and violence, continue to be deluded by these myths. Tripp describes one key myth:

> The so-called national institutions, therefore, on closer inspection revealed themselves to be webs of patron-client networks, sustained by the violence used against those who challenged the system, dispensing the ruler's patronage along lines which gave the lie to the official myth of a distinctive, unifying Iraqi identity.[42]

Saddam ratcheted up his suppression of the Shi'a, and they called for his ouster. In April 1980, the Shi'a attempted to assassinate Tariq Aziz,

Saddam's number-two man. In retaliation, Saddam executed Grand Ayatollah Sayyid Muhammad Baqir al-Sadr, the top Shi'i authority in the world, and his family.

In 1975, an Iraq-Iran border dispute had been settled in Iran's favor, which was stronger at that time; now that Iran was weakened and isolated internationally by revolution, Saddam Hussein wanted to take advantage of that vulnerability and invaded Iran in September 1980. Also, the fundamentalist Shi'i revolution in Iran in 1979 had scared Saddam Hussein and Iraq's minority Sunni ruling elite. They thought this revolution might have appealed to Iraq's Shi'a, which made up a 60 percent majority of the Iraqi population.[43]

The spread of Iran's fundamentalist Islamic revolution and Iran's zealous and effective counterattacks threatened perceived Western interests more than Saddam Hussein's bloodthirsty tyranny, so the United States provided Saddam with helicopters, mortars, and support in logistics, satellite and other intelligence,[44] and military planning (although the Reagan administration sold anti-tank missiles to the Iranians in a naive attempt to get the Iranian-sponsored group Hezbollah to release hostages in Lebanon). U.S. satellite intelligence was key to defeating Iranian counterattacks and conducting a battlefield reversal so that Iraq could go back on a successful offensive in 1988—thus forcing Iran to accept a cease-fire that year. Also, the U.S. Navy actively fought the Iranian navy in the Persian Gulf and destroyed much of it. According to Charles Tripp, the open-ended commitment of U.S. naval forces, effectively fighting on Iraq's side, also was a contributing factor in Iran accepting the cease-fire.[45] The West even sold Saddam armaments and the precursors for chemical and biological weapons. The eight-year Iraq-Iran war was one of the bloodiest of the twentieth century—featuring attacks on each other's cities, Iraqi use of poison gas, and Iranian human-wave assaults. Iraq and Iran lost a staggering 1.5 million men—all for virtually no change in territory between the two sides.

The Sunni Kurds, ever ready to take advantage of the Iraqi government's weakness, revolted again in northern Iraq in the late 1980s during the Iran-Iraq War, helping the Shi'i Iranians against their Sunni-ruled

Arab government.[46] This Kurdish aid to the enemy motivated Saddam to savagely repress and use poison gas against the Kurds, but these horrible actions had little effect on U.S. support for Saddam in his war with Iran. (Ironically, in 2003, the U.S. would invade Iraq, allegedly merely because Saddam was perceived to be reconstituting chemical and other unconventional weapons programs.)

In the south, ethnic origin seemed to have trumped sectarian affiliation during the Iran-Iraq War, as Shi'i Arabs—making up 60 percent of Iraq's population and a majority in the enlisted ranks of Iraq's military—remained loyal to Sunni Arab–dominated Iraq during the war rather than side with their Shi'i brethren in Iran. Some have taken this latter fact to show that at least Arab Iraqis have a national identity, but this only occurred during a war with the Arab world's traditional, external, nearby, and mortal enemy, Iran (and Persia before it). Furthermore, as Tripp observed,

> It is impossible to judge how far the active participation of the Shi'i Iraqis in the war effort was due to their overwhelming sense of their Arab and Iraqi identities. Probably more decisive were pragmatic considerations such as the need to defend themselves against the attacking forces of Iran or the dire consequences for them and their families should they refuse to fight [for the ruthless Saddam].[47]

In 1991, an attack by an outside power from far away—the United States—caused the Shi'a (and Kurds) to revolt against the Sunni regime—not support it—and the current U.S. invasion and occupation also has not unified the two sects in opposition. This Sunni–Shi'i rift in Iraq goes back millennia.

At the end of the eight-year Iran-Iraq War, Saddam Hussein had piled up a large debt. He felt that he had fought the Iranians on behalf of all Arabs and wanted the Arabic Gulf states, including Kuwait, to forgive the debt and reduce oil output so world oil prices would rise—thus netting Iraq more petroleum revenues. Also, Saddam accused Kuwait of slant drilling under Iraq's territory to steal Iraqi oil. In the face of Saddam's threats to Kuwait, the United States made the same mistake it did in Korea in 1950. It implied to a potential aggressor that the United States would not come to the defense of the victim of the potential aggression. In 1950, Secretary of State Dean Acheson had said that South Korea was not included in the U.S. defense perimeter. In 1990, U.S. policy was that America would not get involved in territorial disputes between Arab countries.[48] Both the North Koreans in 1950 and the Iraqis in 1990 read this to mean that the United States would do nothing if they invaded their southern neighbors. If the United States deemed the then-poor South Korea of 1950 and the small Kuwait of 1990 strategic to U.S. security (quite a stretch), U.S. officials should have explicitly tried to deter an attack beforehand rather than implying a green light to the aggressor and then panicking after the hostile invasion occurred.

The second mistake the United States made was to continue its policy tilt toward Iraq during the 1988-to-1990 period—after Iraq came out of the Iran-Iraq War with a military advantage over Iran.

A third mistake was President George H. W. Bush's urging of the Kurds and Shi'a to rise up against Saddam's Sunni government at the end of the first Gulf War. When they did, the United States stood by and let Saddam slaughter them (mirroring what Henry Kissinger had allowed to happen to the Kurdish rebellion in 1975). Bush did not intervene to stop Saddam because the rebellions began to take on an ethno-sectarian nature. The Turks successfully lobbied in Washington against the U.S. supporting the Kurdish rebellion in the north, and the Bush administration did not like the fact that Shi'i Islamist parties returning from exile in Iran were taking over the southern rebellion (ironically, these same Islamist parties now run Iraq, and Bush's son supported them in doing so). President George H. W. Bush feared a weak and fragmented Iraq that could fall into civil war or be ripe for intervention by a local power, such as Iran[49]; however, he should have thought about that again before encouraging the Kurdish and Shi'i rebellions, and his son should have heeded his father's concerns before invading Iraq in 2003. Saddam and previous Iraqi rulers from the minority Sunni group, in a "divide and conquer" tactic, had long used ethno-sectarian divisions within Iraq to maintain Sunni rule. Saddam's repression further exacerbated such ethno-religious fissures.

The world community, in an unsuccessful bid to get Saddam to withdraw his invasion forces from Kuwait, slapped an extremely harsh and comprehensive economic embargo on Iraq. After the United States liberated Kuwait in the first Gulf War, these sanctions were reoriented to weaken Saddam, keep him "in his box," and prevent him from making progress on acquiring chemical, biological, and nuclear weapons. All they really succeeded in doing was making Iraqi citizens poorer and lessening the chance of democracy ever taking root in that country. Add to this the fact that during the first Gulf War, Iraq's army survived but its civilian infrastructure was bombed into rubble.[50]

In a fit of guilt over Saddam's brutal repression of the U.S.-instigated Kurdish and Shi'i revolts, from 1991 to 2003 the United States and Britain created "no fly" zones over northern and southern Iraq, within which Iraqi aircraft were not allowed to fly. In reality, to enforce the no-fly zones, the U.S. and Britain waged a low-level war against Iraq before and after President Bill Clinton launched larger air strikes against Iraq in the 1998 Desert Fox bombing campaign and until the U.S. invasion of Iraq in 2003. During the 1990s, under the northern no-fly-zone protection, the two Kurdish parties—the Kurdistan Democratic Party and the Patriotic Union of Kurdistan—created two separate administrative areas; cultivated Turkey, Iran, and Saddam's Iraqi regime during the open war with each other from 1993 to 1998; and finally reached a power-sharing agreement that gave them effective independence from Baghdad. But Charles Tripp cautioned against using Kurdistan from the end of the first Gulf War in 1991 to the invasion of Iraq in 2003 as a model for the unified democracy Iraq could become:

> The example of Kurdish development during the previous decade or so, both economic and political, was held up as a demonstration of the possibility of establishing an open and plural politics in Iraq. Given the actual record of internecine fighting, clientelism and

corruption behind the façade of representative, plural politics this called for a certain suspension of disbelief.[51]

In sum, all of these wars and economic sanctions did little to heal—and instead exacerbated—the historic cleavages between Sunni Arabs and Kurds and between Sunni and Shi'i Arabs, all of which erupted once again after the United States removed Saddam's iron rule by its 2003 invasion and subsequent ill-fated occupation. William R. Polk, a former State Department official and professor at Harvard and the University of Chicago, said it best: "In the conditions of the [Iraq] war and the [U.S.] occupation, submerged ethnic hostilities have burst into a tragic civil war."[52] A quick review of Iraq's history (as explicated above) would have predicted this outcome. Even if some authors ignore the history and argue that ethno-sectarian cleavages in Iraqi society arose only recently during Saddam's time, and others argue that Iraqi nationalism runs deeper than meets the eye because the Iraqi state—almost one hundred years old—has put down at least some roots, the current intense ethno-sectarian tensions and violence are real, and separating ethno-sectarian populations has reduced them.

Iraq is an artificial country. The Ottoman Turks kept the three provinces of what is now Iraq separate because of their cultural, ethnic, and sectarian differences. The British foolishly combined them and had to struggle to maintain control of the combined, yet fractured, society. The social order was held together only by brutal centralized rule—first by the British and then by a string of Sunni dictators. But in a sign that all was not well under the surface, there were many periodic uprisings by the Kurds and the Shi'a against the brutal Sunni rulers. By this author's count, the Kurds revolted against the Sunni-dominated Iraqi central government in 1920, 1923–1932, 1935–1936, 1945, 1958–1962, 1964–1970, 1972, 1974–1975, and 1991; Shi'i unrest against that same central government occurred in 1920, 1927, 1930–1933, 1935–1936, 1956, 1969, 1974, 1977, and 1991.[53] Thus, when the Bush administration launched its ill-fated invasion and ouster of Saddam Hussein, only the latest strongman, powerful pent-up centrifugal ethno-sectarian forces were unleashed.

Charles Tripp best summarized Iraq's fractured history:

> Neither the state nor those who have commanded it have managed to ensure that the multiple histories of the Iraqis are subsumed into a single narrative of state power. Despite the resources available to them and their sometimes ferocious methods, Iraq's rulers have had little success in forcing the histories of Iraq's various communities to conform with their own timetables and objectives. Indeed, the logic of political survival has often dictated otherwise. The exploitation of fracture lines within the population and restrictive understandings of political trust have kept hierarchies of status and privilege intact, subverting the very idea of a national community in whose name successive governments have claimed to act.[54]

The Current Mess

Unfortunately, the Bush administration's forte was expansive neoconservative ideology and not Iraq's history. During its occupation, the Bush administration further exacerbated ethno-sectarian fissures in Iraq. In its ideological obsession with seeing foreign peoples with purple thumbs, the administration held an Iraqi election in 2005 that ultimately focused on ethnicity rather than policy—thus actually sharpening the divisions that created separate, defensible, and homogeneous areas in many major cities, such as Baghdad, Mosul, Baquba, Basra, and Kirkuk.

Furthermore, the administration armed and trained the Iraqi security forces—mainly consisting of Kurdish and Shi'i militia members with greater loyalty to their groups than to Iraq—but then became desperate to quell the decentralized (like everything else in Iraq) Sunni insurgency. Thus it began buying off many of those Sunni guerrillas by paying, arming, and training them.

The Shi'i-dominated Iraqi government, unhappy with U.S. training and arming of these "awakening" Sunnis, was slow to integrate them into the Iraqi security forces and even tried to arrest many of their leaders. Although reducing the violence until President Bush left office, these new armed Sunni militias will make the likely future full-blown civil war that much bloodier. If something isn't done, all of these varying U.S.-trained forces will probably eventually fight each other. Add to this tribal and village forces and Turkmen, Yazidi, and Assyrian militias. In fact so many different armed groups exist that Iraq has been turned into a Somalia-like aggregation of city-states run by warlords, and trying to disarm all of these armies would be futile. The only alternative is to accept reality and recognize a decentralized Iraq—with security and most other government functions being provided at the local level.

The current Iraqi Constitution, adopted in October 2005 by the Shi'a and Kurds over Sunni objections, allows some decentralization but would probably have to be modified to maximize such devolution of power to local and regional governments. The constitution vaguely calls for a federal, democratic, parliamentary, and republican form of government and a "single independent federal state." The document left the relationship between the central and local governments undefined, and also the distribution of oil revenues. In October 2006, Iraq's national assembly voted for a law that would allow all of the nation's eighteen provinces to have votes on whether to combine into larger Kurdistan-like regions.[55] The decentralization may have to be greater and should not use the old artificial provincial boundaries, but should be based on how the Iraqis themselves want to devolve authority. Also, democratic governance in some areas may have to be sacrificed for stability.

Had the Bush administration read the history of Iraq or consulted Arabist scholars, it might have more wisely concluded that fractious Iraq was one of the least likely countries in the Middle East to accept a unified, democratic federation from the top down at gunpoint. In contrast, Stansfield observed that states in the Middle East with homogeneous populations haven't had their legitimacy questioned the way Iraq has had its challenged. In addition, he noted that comparative evidence should have predicted that even under best-case scenarios, democracy would be harder to achieve in Iraq than other places because of the lack of prerequisite building blocks, such as a democratic political culture, a united democratic will, and genuine political parties. Reducing even further the chance that democratization might work, the Bush administration was committed to imposing democracy through Iraqi exile groups with little political standing in Iraq and ignored the need to foster democracy from the bottom up in existing indigenous ethno-sectarian and tribal communities.[56]

Having pledged to withdraw U.S. forces from Iraq, the Obama administration is now faced with cleaning up the mess left by the Bush administration.

2

The Current Instability in Iraq

THE UNITED STATES has plunged into an Iraqi quagmire.
The nation's swashbuckling victory in the first Gulf War led to the most
egregious sins that can be made in military affairs—hubris and underes-
timation of the enemy. The U.S. and Soviet superpowers made the same
mistake respectively in Vietnam in the 1960s and 1970s and in Afghanistan in the 1980s. But as those dilemmas dried up in memory, U.S. government officials in Iraq apparently had to relearn the same lessons.

Historically, guerrilla operations by the weak against the strong have
proved very effective. Guerrillas take advantage of sanctuaries offered
by terrain (for example, thick jungles, high mountains, or densely
populated cities) to launch hit-and-run attacks against small or isolated
groups of the stronger party's forces. They then blend back into their sur-
roundings, pretending to be ordinary citizens. In fact, according to William R. Polk, who has studied many instances of guerrilla warfare, the
guerrillas almost always win in the longterm unless the foreign power is
willing to commit genocide—something a liberal democracy such as the
United States cannot and should not stomach.[57]

In Iraq, after a second swift conventional victory, U.S. overconfidence
reigned. A uniformed President Bush stood on a U.S. aircraft carrier in
triumph before a banner proclaiming "Mission Accomplished." That
bravado quickly evaporated in what looks to have been a preplanned
guerrilla insurgency, designed with the long-term goal of getting the
superpower out of Iraq. The vast majority of U.S. deaths have occurred
after the "cessation of major combat operations."

Even during the successful conventional phase of this second U.S.-Iraq war, harbingers of doom arose but were ignored. Guerrilla tactics by Saddam Hussein's fedayeen fighters disrupted U.S. supply lines during the advance to Baghdad. Eric Shinseki, the army chief of staff, was apparently one of the few senior U.S. government officials to realize that the occupation phase of the Iraq campaign might end up being as difficult or more difficult than the initial invasion. Top Bush administration defense officials, however, ridiculed Shinseki's warning that hundreds of thousands of U.S. ground forces would be required to occupy Iraq.[58] Perhaps these hawkish civilian officials should have paid more attention to an expert on ground combat. (But even a much larger force would have had problems subduing a nation the size of California in which a majority of the people have never regarded the foreign invasion as "liberation.")[59]

Iraq Is Not Post–World War II Japan or Germany

Those officials also should have paid attention to analysts who disputed the administration's claim that "liberating" Iraq would resemble the post–World War II U.S. occupations in Japan and Germany. For example, John Dower, an award-winning historian of modern Japan, maintains that "almost everything that abetted stability and serious reform in postwar Japan is conspicuously absent in the case of Iraq."[60] Before being destroyed in World War II, Japan and Germany had the social and economic organization and the highly skilled work forces of developed nations. More important, they also had unified societies, at least some experience with democracy, and an external threat (the Soviet Union) that had the potential to be worse for them than the U.S. occupation. Iraq has none of those characteristics.[61] It is a fractious developing country with little prior experience in genuine democracy, a social fabric torn by three recent wars and more than a decade of the most stringent economic isolation in world history, and no potentially hegemonic external enemy.

Going from Bad to Worse

Surprisingly, the U.S. position in Iraq remains bad and is bound to get worse. Violent attacks continue, and the situation has included lawlessness, a prostrate economy, shortages of basic services (such as electricity and clean water), U.S. torture and censorship of the Iraqi press, U.S. cancellation of local Iraqi elections because anti–U.S. Islamists and Saddam loyalists would likely have won,[62] and U.S. pilfering of Iraqi funds to give U.S. companies sweetheart deals. All of these factors have made the continuing U.S. occupation more and more unpopular with Iraqis.

Also, with attacks on Iraqi security forces a prominent tactic of the remaining insurgency, people remain somewhat skittish about signing up. More important, the loyalty, competence, and reliability of those who do sign up are questionable and make many of these forces more sympathetic to their ethno-sectarian roots than to Iraq as a nation.

Years after the end of the conventional phase of the war, U.S. intelligence on the enemy is so poor that "victory" in the long term is unlikely—despite a reduction of violence in the country. Knowing how to fight an enemy about whom you know very little is difficult. Even though the U.S. military is taking casualties at lower rates than are the insurgents, the same thing happened in Vietnam. The Vietnamese guerrillas, fighting for their Southeast Asian homeland, were willing to take many more casualties than the United States and to wait for the casualty-averse superpower to become exhausted and go home. The Iraqi militias and insurgents are likely to be willing to do the same and appear to be doing just that. And they may not have to wait all that long.

Recently, even the Bush administration agreed to withdraw all combat forces from Iraq by the end of 2011. Considering the outcome of the U.S. presidential election, that withdrawal could be moved to an earlier time. With today's twenty-four-hour news, the Iraq war became unpopular in the United States in little more than a year (as of the summer of 2004, 56 percent of the American people believed invading Iraq was a mistake[63]). It took years for the Vietnam War to lose public support.[64]

Thus, as in Vietnam, the U.S. might win every battle and still lose the war—not an uncommon outcome for the strong in guerilla warfare.

According to Seymour Hersh of *The New Yorker,* a former Israeli intelligence official told him that the Israeli leadership had concluded as early as August 2003 that the U.S. situation in Iraq could not be rescued. As a result, the Israelis expanded military training of Kurdish militias in an attempt to salvage an independent Kurdistan with access to Kirkuk's oil.[65]

Resistance movements usually need three important elements to succeed: sanctuary, outside assistance, and, most important, support of the indigenous people. In the urban Iraqi landscape, militias, using hit-and-run tactics, can melt back into the general population—thus foiling U.S. forces' attempts to neutralize them. Also, Iraqi militias are getting money and weapons through Iraq's porous borders with neighboring countries; Shi'i militias are being funded, armed, and trained by Iran. Some assistance is undoubtedly coming from the inflamed worldwide Islamist jihad movement, but some may also be coming covertly from the governments of Syria, Jordan, and Saudi Arabia. But little outside military assistance is needed, because unlike in past insurgencies elsewhere, Iraq is awash with enough arms for the militias to fight on for many years.

Finally, the guerrillas draw public support from a well of ill feeling toward the foreign occupier. It is no wonder that, after leading the most grinding international economic sanctions in history and two wars against Iraq, the U.S. occupiers were not greeted with flowers. (Estimates of Iraqi children who died as a result of the U.S.–led United Nations [UN] embargo range from 227,000 to 500,000.)[66] The U.S. occupation authority's own polls showed that 92 percent of Iraqis thought of U.S. forces as occupiers, whereas only 2 percent believed they were liberators.[67] Most Iraqis want the United States to leave Iraq, even if security becomes worse than at present. These low approval ratings will likely dip even further as the U.S. occupation drags on.

Oil production and exports remain anemic, unemployment is at 30 to 50 percent, and electricity and clean water can be had only sporadically. Iraqi funds have been used to give U.S. defense contractors non-competitive sweetheart deals—for example, the monopoly contract that Halliburton received for postwar reconstruction.[68] How can the perception be anything but that the United States is looting Iraq's oil resources? All of these factors make the continuing U.S. occupation unpopular in Iraq.

Most independent military and intelligence experts thought that the Bush administration led the United States into strategic folly. For example, Senator Chuck Hagel, a Republican on the Foreign Relations and Intelligence committees, said, "The fact is, we're in trouble. We're in deep trouble in Iraq." Republican senator Richard Lugar, chairman of the Foreign Relations Committee, expressed similar sentiments.[69] General Anthony Zinni, a former marine commander of U.S. forces in the Middle East, noted, "And to think that we are going to 'stay the course,' the course is headed over Niagara Falls."[70] Similarly, testifying before the Senate Foreign Relations Committee, marine general Joseph Hoar, another former U.S. Middle East commander, said, "I believe we are absolutely on the brink of failure. We are looking into the abyss." In a surprisingly candid assessment from an active senior officer back from Iraq, Major General Charles H. Swannack Jr., commander of the army's Eighty-second Airborne Division, noted, "We are winning tactically, but have made a few tactical blunders . . . which created strategic consequences in world opinion. We are losing public support regionally, internationally, and within America—thus, currently, we are losing strategically."[71] After Condoleezza Rice, the president's national security advisor, recruited Larry Diamond, a civilian scholar at Stanford University's conservative Hoover Institution, to go to Iraq and be a high-level advisor to the U.S. Coalition Provisional Authority, he rendered an even starker analysis. According to Diamond, not only was the United States losing the war, but the whole enterprise has been counterproductive to U.S. security: "Iraq is more dangerous to the U.S. potentially than it was at the moment we went to war." He continued, "A country not an imminent threat to the security of the U.S. is now in some areas a haven of the most murderous, dedicated enemies of the U.S., including al Qaeda."[72]

Since the U.S. troop surge in 2007 and 2008, insurgent violence has been reduced but remains at high levels. Rather than the U.S. troop surge, the primary cause of the reduction has been the United States buying off the Sunni insurgents by paying, arming, and training them. Also, the U.S. is the beneficiary of a fragile cease-fire with the Shi'i Mahdi Army militia and is working with the militia in some Shi'i areas to provide aid and services. As noted earlier, this strategy will reduce violence in the short term and presented a better face during the U.S. presidential election, but it will probably make the likely future full-blown civil war worse by arming more of the contestants.

In addition, the Shi'i-dominated government has promised to integrate some of the former Sunni guerrillas (the Sunni Awakening) into the Iraqi security forces, but there has been resistance to doing this and the government has actually arrested a significant number of Awakening leaders. These unfortunate policies could be a flashpoint for the renewal of more severe violence. Finally, Kirkuk, a city near the second-largest oil reserves in Iraq, could be a field for future violent competition over control of the city and such resources. More widely in Iraq, splitting Iraq's oil wealth could very well prove extremely contentious.

A way must be found to permanently reduce the violence and give Iraq the best chance of stability and prosperity in the long term. Even though violence has been reduced, the armed groups may very well be waiting until the U.S. leaves to resume the civil war. Given the hole that the Bush administration has dug for the United States in Iraq, achieving a secure outcome will not be easy. According to Diamond, "There are really no good options."[73] In this report, however, I propose a solution that may prove to be the Obama administration's best chance of salvaging the situation.

Root Causes of the Violence

To reduce the violence in Iraq over the long term, its root causes must be uncovered. The Iraqi insurgents appear to be fighting for two main reasons. The first is to get the foreign invader out of Iraq. Zbigniew

Brzezinski, President Carter's national security advisor, warned that a continued U.S. occupation would result in more zealous Iraqi hostility.[74] The Bush administration blamed the violence on criminals, former Saddam loyalists, and foreign jihadists, but those populations have always been limited. The ongoing guerrilla war appears to indicate that average Iraqis perceive that they are defending their homeland against a foreign invader. For example, the militia of Shi'i cleric Moqtada al-Sadr appears to fit into none of Bush's categories.

It is not surprising that patriotic feelings have arisen in the face of an unnecessary U.S. invasion that appears neocolonial in nature. (If the United States were to be invaded by a foreign power, similar patriotic feelings among Americans would probably ignite and lead to armed resistance.) Furthermore, according to the tenets of Islam, if Islamic territory is attacked by non-Muslims, every Muslim's duty is to fight back in any way possible; it is considered a sin not to do so.[75] Even moderate Muslims have this belief in "defensive jihad." That conviction led Muslims from all over the world to flock to Afghanistan during the 1980s to oppose the Soviet "infidel" invaders. It also has fueled the fierce resistance that Chechens and foreign Islamic fighters have waged against the perceived Russian occupiers in Chechnya.

Given the Islamic faith's belief in defensive jihad, the Bush administration's conduct of the post-9/11 "war on terror," including the very visible invasions of Afghanistan and Iraq, has been the worst possible course of action. Although most Muslims disagree with Osama bin Laden's killing of innocents, many believe he is waging a justifiable defensive jihad against an infidel U.S. superpower that militarily occupies Muslim-inhabited areas or supports corrupt, secular governments in Islamic lands, including the territory containing the holiest sites in Islam—Saudi Arabia. After the September 11 attacks, the Bush administration reflexively inflamed the Islamic world further and inadvertently raised bin Laden's stature in it by conducting a much too visible war in Afghanistan and an unnecessary invasion of Iraq.

Al Qaeda sanctuaries in Taliban-controlled Afghanistan clearly had to be eradicated. But domestic political pressure on President George

W. Bush to show that he was avenging the horrible September 11 attacks thus caused the war to be waged far too visibly in a Muslim land. In the end, the Bush administration let bin Laden get away by not pursuing him covertly and aggressively enough with U.S. forces, while roiling an already inflamed Islamic world with a very visible war—the worst possible outcome for the United States. Furthermore, "infidel" U.S. forces have continued to occupy Afghan territory long after they ousted the Taliban, strengthening al Qaeda and the Taliban in Afghanistan and now in Pakistan.

The Bush administration's snafu in Afghanistan might be excused by its good intentions in going after the sanctuary of terrorists who attacked the U.S. homeland, but the monumental blunder of using the September 11 attacks to settle old scores with Iraq is unforgivable. The 9/11 Commission stated that they saw no evidence of a "collaborative operational relationship" between Iraq and al Qaeda or that Iraq had helped al Qaeda attack the United States.[76] Invading another Muslim land for no justifiable reason stoked worldwide Islamic hatred of the United States much more than did the initial war in Afghanistan, which the Islamic world perceived as more legitimate.

Most groups in Iraq hate the idea of a long-term U.S. military occupation of their country. If some sort of international force that had not invaded the country and that was predominantly Muslim—thus increasing somewhat the legitimacy of the occupation—were to replace U.S. troops, violence in that country would likely be reduced even more. Most other Muslim countries, however, will not provide forces to help stabilize Iraq as long as U.S. forces remain there.

A second reason opposition groups in Iraq—both Sunni and Shi'i— are fighting is for their place in a post–U.S. Iraq. First, the Sunnis (20 percent of the Iraqi population), the traditional rulers of Iraq, are fighting because they fear harsh paybacks (already being doled out) from a majority Shi'i (60 percent of the population) central government. Sunnis gained the impression that they were being punished for the excesses of Saddam's regime when the ruling Baath Party was dissolved, when party members were stripped of their positions in the military and civil society, and when indigenous Sunnis were excluded from the Iraqi Governing Council in favor of Sunni exiles or Kurds. (The secular Sunnis are made up of several groups and some [the Awakening] have been paid by the U.S. to quit fighting, while Sunni Islamists, such as al Qaeda in Iraq, remain recalcitrant.) Also, the Shi'i Mahdi militia under Moqtada al-Sadr consists of radical Islamists who fear being marginalized in a post–U.S. Iraq controlled by other fairly radical Shi'i groups (Dawa and the Supreme Islamic Iraqi Council). Al-Sadr's forces have fought U.S. forces and their client Iraqi government's militias (sometimes in the guise of Iraqi security forces), but they may be battling harder in the future if a suitable political settlement is not reached that allows each faction to largely control its own area.

Finally, the non-Arab Sunni Kurds (20 percent of the population), with their own well-armed militias (the rival Kurdistan Democratic Party and Patriotic Union of Kurdistan), are not yet fighting the other groups or amongst themselves, but they have made it clear that they too want to avoid oppression by a Shi'i central government. Kurdish peoples are currently minorities in four states—Iraq, Iran, Syria, and Turkey—and historically have been oppressed by all of them. Thus the Iraqi Kurds—leery of future oppression from the Shi'a—want to retain the de facto autonomy, democratic government, economic prosperity, and intensified sense of ethnic identity that they have enjoyed for almost two decades. And, most likely, they will want to move toward an independent Kurdish state.[77] Every poll taken in Iraqi Kurdistan indicates that the overwhelming majority of Kurds desire independence; however, the Iraqi Kurdish leadership is aware of apprehension in Turkey (because an independent Iraqi Kurdistan could be a beacon for separatist tendencies among Turkish Kurds) and the international community (because of the possibility of a Turkish invasion of Iraqi Kurdistan over Iraqi Kurdish independence) about such an immediate move. Furthermore, like the wealthier Czechs in Czechoslovakia and the richer Slovenes and Croats in Yugoslavia, the Iraqi Kurdish population—whose average income is 25 percent higher than the rest of Iraq—is unlikely to be receptive to continuing to subsidize the poorer ethno-sectarian groups in the society.[78]

According to a 2004 report by Chatham House, a respected British research institute, each of the three ethno-sectarian groups has an "exclusivist" vision for a future Iraq: the Shi'a in southern Iraq are on a trajectory to an Islamic state, and little support for secular parties exists there; the Sunnis are traveling the path of secular Arab nationalism; and the Kurds, who have had their own de facto state for almost two decades, likely want to make it permanent, and do not like the other groups' goals. The U.S. occupation authority has found that many within these obstreperous groups are attempting to thwart the formation of a central government.

Since the British created the fiction of "Iraq" in the 1920s, the country has seen only autocratic governments and so has no experience with true democracy.[79] In Saddam's Iraq, as in other authoritarian countries in the Arab world, the only dissent permitted was in the mosques, thus giving the Islamic religion enormous prestige and legitimacy. Although the Shi'a may want to subject all Iraqis to Islamic governance, even they have separatist tendencies. In the south, they control a majority of Iraq's oil resources and will not want those revenues diffused to other parts of Iraq.[80] Even the Sunnis, who have few documented oil reserves in the middle section of Iraq, are becoming more separatist because of suspicions of Shi'i control of a central government—this due to the brutal ethnic cleansing to which the Sunnis have been subjected. In the north, the Kurds also have oil and are the most eager to govern themselves without the help of Baghdad.

The Chatham report said that although some Iraqis put their national identity before their group affiliation and that these Iraqis might even be in the majority in Iraq, "grass roots power is currently in the hands of those groups which assert themselves according to their communal identity."[81] Also, in many such chaotic situations, the opinions of armed and well-organized minorities win out over the wishes of the majority— for example, in the Bolshevik Revolution in Russia. In particular, the Kurds have a stronger militia than either the Shi'a or Sunnis and are also more exclusivist than those populations. However, Chatham's optimistic conclusion about the strength of Iraqi national identity may be out-dated after several years of severe sectarian violence and ethnic cleansing between Arab Sunnis and Shi'a.

Why a Centralized Iraq Is Not Viable

President Bush promised a "free, unified Iraq." The United States would like to remake Iraq in the U.S. image of a liberal federated repub-lic. Iraq's constitution does create a federal state, but no agreement among Iraqis exists on what this means. Circumstances on the ground make it unlikely that such an Iraqi federal state will come to fruition.[82]

Federation Versus Confederation

Federation as a form of government is revered in the United States in part because the United States largely invented it. Australia, Canada, and Switzerland are other modern examples of federations.

A federation is usually defined as a combination of shared rule and self-rule. The central government and state governments directly rule citizens in the same territory, but somewhat independently—that is, in different spheres of citizens' lives. (In areas of overlapping jurisdiction, the central government usually has supremacy over state governments.)[83] For example, the central government will handle foreign affairs, defense, immigration, economic matters that benefit from standard regulation, and activities that physically cross state borders.[84] The powers of the cen-tral government and of the states are usually guaranteed by a constitution that can be amended by some sort of majority (that is, non-unanimity) of state governments. The central government cannot dismiss a state gov-ernment or governments. Neither secession by a state government, nor the state government's nullification of the central government's legisla-tion, is permitted.[85] Also, the key power of taxation is shared between the two levels of government.[86]

In contrast, a confederation government interacts mainly with the state governments and does not rule citizens directly.[87] In this system, the states, rather than the central government, have most of the power. A confederation government consists only of institutions that the state governments have agreed to share among themselves.[88] The European Union is an example of a confederation.

An Iraqi Federation Is Unlikely to Be Successful

Because each of Iraq's ethnic and sectarian factions—most of them with armed militias—is suspicious that a strong Iraqi central government might be controlled by a hostile rival group or groups, any attempt by an outside authority to impose a federation might very well end in a full-blown civil war.

Iraq is an artificial state,[89] created when the British combined three provinces of the defunct Ottoman Empire;[90] the three areas had never been united politically, had no feeling of collective nationality, and contained three major ethno-sectarian and other minor groups, subdivided by tribal loyalties. This situation has made the Iraqi state dysfunctional from the start, its unruly populace held together in one country by the brute force of arms. In fact, it was the hatred and distrust among the groups and their inability to work together in any natural unified political arrangement that made authoritarianism possible.[91] Saddam Hussein and his family (part of a tribe that was a minority in the Sunni ruling class)—like the Ottomans and British rulers before them—exploited these ethnic fissures to retain control over the country. Although Saddam was able to divide the groups (more accurately, he simply exacerbated the existing divisions) for his own gain, he failed to "conquer" them by imposing a homogeneous political culture on them.[92]

Unless the U.S. government is willing to tolerate a return to such brutal autocratic oppression (given the current dysfunctional state of affairs, it might eventually be tempted by that option in order to restore some semblance of stability), the same natural centrifugal forces will likely pull Iraq apart. After the dissolution of the Soviet Union and the Warsaw Pact, both the Czech and Slovak publics were initially against partition, but their leaders eventually led them down the road to separation.[93] It is probably inevitable that the leaders of various factions in Iraq will do the same. The question remains whether partition would be a peaceful, planned road to gradual separation (or decentralization), as in the case of Czechoslovakia, or an unruly split after a bloody civil war, as in the case of Yugoslavia.

Despite upbeat public pronouncements by the Bush administration on progress in remolding Iraq, a highly classified national intelligence estimate written for President Bush was pessimistic about the outcome. The estimate postulated three alternative scenarios—the worst being civil war and the best being an Iraq in which security and political and economic stability remain in doubt.[94] According to David Ignatius of the *Washington Post,* the Iraq situation might eventually spiral into a super-Lebanese civil war.[95] So much for the Bush administration's plan to create an Iraqi democracy that will remake the Middle East in the U.S. image—an outcome that most experts in the region have always thought was a stretch.

Similarly, an even more downbeat report from Chatham House in 2004 stated that the fragmentation of Iraq "is, sadly, a not unlikely scenario." The think tank predicted:

> The Fragmentation Scenario represents what will happen if competing elements and interests in Iraq fail to cohere. . . .
>
> Essentially this is the default scenario, in the sense that it best describes the tendencies at work that have to be overcome in order to avoid fragmentation. . . .
>
> Antipathy to the U.S. presence grows, not so much in a unified Iraqi nationalist backlash, but rather in a fragmented manner that could presage civil war if the U.S. cuts and runs. Even if U.S. forces try to hold out and prop up the central authority it may still lose control.[96]

As prognosticated by Chatham House, Iraq has fragmented into an aggregation of city-states run by warlords with militias. Chatham House predicted a civil war if the United States "cuts and runs" (a characterization it does not define), but did not seem to be much more optimistic if the U.S. forces stayed. Thus if a continued U.S. occupation does not greatly increase the chances of a positive outcome—or, as I believe, most likely diminishes such chances—it would be better for the United States to withdraw its forces and save lives, hundreds of billions of dollars, and its prestige. Similarly, during the Vietnam War, arguments were made that U.S. lives and billions of taxpayer dollars had to be spent in the deepening quagmire to preserve U.S. "credibility," but the United States would have retained more of all three had it withdrawn U.S. forces much earlier.

"Cutting and running" is too harsh a description of a possible U.S. exit from Iraq, however. This is especially true if the United States, before leaving, sets up a mechanism that gives Iraqis the best chance for peace and prosperity in the long term—decentralized governance and genuine self-determination, probably within a confederation of various ethnic and sectarian enclaves.

Trying a federated middle ground in Iraq would probably not work. It failed in Czechoslovakia. As in this case, varying economic situations among the subnational groupings would probably endanger a federation's social cohesion.[97] Also, creating a successful federation is much more likely with a preexisting congenial and tolerant political culture[98] and with the common vision and mutual trust required for shared institutions,[99] all of which are missing in Iraq. Furthermore, according to Professor Clement Dodd, formerly at the University of London, "Federations made from the top down, where there is change from a unitary state, are less stable than those that are made from the bottom upwards: there is likely to be more enthusiasm for the new configuration in the latter than in the former case."[100] In other words, liberal federated government is better created by the bubbling up of desire from the people than by a foreign power's imposition of it from above on a reluctant populace—as in the case of Iraq.

Federations have historically been unsuccessful in polities containing fractious ethnic, racial, sectarian, regional, or other groupings. The late Professor Daniel J. Elazar at Temple University, who was a prominent authority on federalism, needs to be quoted at length on why such societal divisions make successful federations difficult:

> Ethnic nationalism is probably the strongest force against federalism. Federalism has become a very popular "solution" for problems of ethnic conflict in public discourse. In fact, ethnic federations are among the most difficult of all to sustain and are the least likely to survive because constituent units based on ethnic nationalisms normally do not want to merge into the kind of tight-knit units necessary for federation. It may be that confederations of ethnic states have a better chance of success. Ethnic federations run the risk of civil war, while ethnic confederations run the risk of secession. . . . Federal theory calls for nationalism on the basis of consent whatever its demographic content, consent which allows both for the division and sharing of powers. Most of today's nationalisms, on the other hand, emphasize those things which separate peoples: language, religion, national myths, or whatever. . . . In general, nineteenth-century-style ethnic nationalism tends to subordinate all free government to its uncompromising position. Federalism is a democratic middle way requiring negotiation and compromise. All aspects of society fostering uncompromising positions make federalism more difficult, if not impossible.[101]

In another work, Elazar cites Nazism, fascism, communism, and even the French Revolution to argue that ideology rarely triumphs over existing ethnic identities.[102] Thus in the absence of an oppressive Iraqi dictatorship that suppresses all ethno-sectarian groups (and maybe even if the United States makes a desperate attempt to reinstate one), the various factions—especially if they are armed—will probably pull apart any externally imposed federation.

Restructuring Iraq at the Point of a Gun Will Not Work

The Iraqi army and other security forces were dismantled early in the U.S. military occupation and have been replaced with newly organized forces. A significant portion of the old security forces became disaffected with their dissolution and took up arms on the side of the resistance. With new replacements for the Iraqi security forces, a continuing insurgency, many other groups armed to the teeth, and Bush administration promises to bring democracy to Iraq and the Middle East, the United States will be hard pressed to reinstate autocratic, centralized rule even if that were the only perceived way of restoring stability. After a can of worms has been opened, it is difficult to get them to crawl back into the container.

Where national identity is weak and no tradition of political pluralism exists, suspicions among rival groups that one group or a band of groups will take over any federal government are likely to prevail and lead to the disintegration of a federation. As mentioned previously, that breakup can be either peaceful or violent. With Iraq awash in weapons, violence, and contentious groups, the breakup of any federation might very well lead to an all-out civil war.

Of course, any U.S.–imposed federation could be propped up by the continued presence of U.S. military forces. Yet if the U.S. government chooses this option, it will probably become stuck in an endless Vietnam-style quagmire. Most Iraqis want U.S. forces to leave. A long occupation would probably fuel more anti–U.S. animosity and cause the number and severity of attacks on the foreign occupier to eventually increase again. The longer the occupation lasts, the less likely the United States is to "win" its counterinsurgency campaign—on which the viability of the U.S.–imposed federation depends. Right now the U.S. has pledged to completely withdraw its forces from Iraq by the end of 2011, but the lure of permanent military bases near the Persian Gulf may cause this agreement with the Iraqis to be amended later.

The U.S. military is already faced with a "half-in and half-out" Vietnam-like situation. Guerrilla wars are often as much or more political than they are military, and the U.S. armed forces, even after Vietnam, are only now mastering the art of fighting them. The U.S. military had a dilemma in Iraq, as its actions in the Sunni city of Fallujah and in the southern Shi'i towns indicated. It could use overwhelming firepower and alienate the all-important hearts and minds of the Iraqi people—as occurred in Vietnam—or it could hold back, appear weak, and let the insurgency continue. Initially, in Iraq, the United States vacillated between the two alternatives. In May 2004, a leaked British memo noted that to reduce anti-American violence, U.S. forces needed to use greater restraint.[103] Similarly, some of the officers commanding other national contingents of the U.S.–led occupation force complained of overly aggressive U.S. military tactics.[104] (Some of these nations had more experience in peacekeeping than the United States.)

The United States allowed Fallujah in the north to be controlled by the Sunni insurgents for many months, then changed tactics and used heavy firepower to blow the town to pieces and permitted the radical Shi'i cleric Moqtada al-Sadr in the south to remain alive and in charge of his still viable militia. Since then, the U.S. has decided more can be obtained with sugar than with vinegar. It has bought off Sunni guerrillas and "made nice" with al-Sadr's militia.

As in Vietnam in the 1970s, in Lebanon in the 1980s, and in Somalia in the 1990s, the goal of most Iraqi groups seems to be to wait until the superpower gets tired and goes home. As noted earlier, because of twenty-four-hour cable news and the Vietnam experience, the American public has soured on this war much more quickly than it did on the conflict in Southeast Asia.

U.S. Strategic Considerations

Despite the U.S. government's rhetoric about letting the Iraqis determine their future, many U.S. officials fear that a decentralized Iraq—what true self-determination would probably produce—would induce "instability" in the Persian Gulf oil patch or result in enemies of the

United States gaining more influence there. The fear that Iran will win influence with the Iraqi Shi'a has already been mentioned here. Syria might also try to dominate some parts of a decentralized Iraq. But why should the United States care so much about Iraq and the Persian Gulf?

Most U.S. "strategic considerations" in the Middle East revolve around ensuring Israel's security and the fear that supplies of oil to the United States from the gulf will be put at risk. Israel, however, is now at peace with many of its Arab neighbors—including Egypt, the most powerful of its potential enemies. Also, the Israelis reportedly have several hundred nuclear weapons, which should deter threats to the nation's survival. Most important, a decentralized Iraq would be less threatening to Israel than a unified one ruled by a strict Islamic Shi'i government.

As for oil, contrary to conventional wisdom, Persian Gulf countries need to sell oil more than the United States needs to buy it. Oil makes up the following percentage of exports from the Gulf nations: Iraq, 90 percent or more; Saudi Arabia, 90–95 percent; Kuwait, 90–95 percent; Iran, 80 percent; Oman, 75 percent; United Arab Emirates, 70 percent; Bahrain, 65 percent;[105] and Qatar, 75–80 percent.[106] Most Gulf states have little else to export. In contrast, oil makes up only approximately 7 percent of U.S. imports.[107] Despite the existence of the Organization of Petroleum Exporting Countries (OPEC) cartel, a worldwide market for oil does function, and OPEC has little control over the long-term price of oil. Economists agree that cartels have not been very effective in keeping the prices of commodities high in the long run. In fact, in the summer of 2004, increased worldwide demand pushed oil prices up further than OPEC would have liked. OPEC was pumping at maximum capacity to attempt to reduce the price. The reason for that counterintuitive behavior is that when the oil price reaches a certain level, alternative energy sources may become cost effective, spurring research that might permanently reduce the long-term demand for the OPEC cartel's key export. High oil prices can also spur "sticky" (not easily reversed) increases in conservation measures by consumers that can have a similar effect. So the market provides a natural restraint on oil prices in the long run. In contrast, war, or the threat of it, usually leads to skyrocketing oil prices.

Even when oil prices are periodically high, however, the adverse economic effects are vastly overstated. Perennial fears of the dire economic effects of oil shortages or price spikes originated in the 1973 "oil crisis." The economic stagflation of the late 1970s was falsely attributed to rising oil prices. The truth is that bad economic policies adopted by the U.S. government—for example, price controls and excessively lax monetary policy—were more to blame than high oil prices. In fact, economist Douglas Bohi has estimated that the petroleum shocks of the 1970s reduced the U.S. gross domestic product (GDP) by only 0.35 percent.[108] More recently, although Germany faced a crude oil price increase of 211 percent between the fourth quarter of 1998 and the third quarter of 2000, it experienced economic growth with falling unemployment and inflation.[109] From 2006 to 2008, oil prices hit new highs, but the U.S. economy did not go into recession until the mortgage meltdown occurred.

The irony is that while U.S. policymakers invest so much time worrying about "critical" supplies of imported crude oil and spend tens of billions of dollars a year to "defend" them with U.S. forces in the Persian Gulf, they are paying much less attention to other seemingly critical inputs to the U.S. economy. For example, imported crude oil is refined into gasoline, jet fuel, and diesel fuel using rare platinum-group metals (platinum and palladium) as catalysts. During the more threatening period of the Cold War, only two countries accounted for almost all of the worldwide mine production of these metals—the Soviet Union (49 percent), the main U.S. rival, and South Africa (46 percent), an unstable country under international economic sanctions for its racial apartheid system. At that time, South Africa held 89 percent of the world's reserve base (minerals still in the ground that are currently and potentially economical to mine) and accounted for 46 percent of U.S. imports.[110] Yet safeguarding South African platinum-group metals using military power was never discussed, and there was even some discussion about banning U.S. imports of such metals to protest South African apartheid.

Similarly, the United States spends almost $200 billion a year on semiconductors—a product that, like oil, is crucial to the U.S. economy and national security.[111] The United States imports roughly 20 percent of its oil from the Persian Gulf.[112] It imports approximately 80 percent of its semiconductors from East Asia.[113] Yet official Washington never worries about shortages or high prices for East Asian circuits and does not justify spending hundreds of billions of dollars a year on military power to make supplies of circuits secure.

Oil is strategic in the narrow sense that it is used for U.S. military forces, but so are semiconductors. Domestically, the U.S. produces thirteen times the annual amount of oil needed to run U.S. military forces.

If the U.S. government's worry about the security of Persian Gulf oil is therefore unnecessary, then consternation about the Iraqi portion of it is even more misplaced. Thus what happens in Iraq—outside of the deaths of U.S. service personnel and Iraqis—is much less important than U.S. policymakers and the public believe. If the strategic elephant in the room—excessive U.S. government concerns about oil supplies— were to evaporate, the United States would have the luxury of allowing the Iraqis complete and genuine self-determination.

3

The Best Alternatives

Partition or Confederation

THE BUSH ADMINISTRATION had the naive belief that the United States could pop the autocratic top off a fractious country the size of California, be greeted as a liberator, subdue the country easily, and convert a nation with no prior experience with democracy into a U.S.–style liberal federated republic. The administration is now mired in an open-ended counterinsurgency in an unfriendly country and has little chance of achieving its grandiose goal. Given this bungling, no perfect solution exists. Almost any policy option has drawbacks. But the alternative with the best chance of success would involve withdrawing U.S. forces rapidly, accepting Iraq's complicated nature, and allowing Iraqis to have genuine self-determination that would probably result in an extremely decentralized government.

Up until this point, the arguments presented against a federation have been utilitarian—that is, federations usually fail when strong ethnic or religious groups exist in the polity. But if the Iraqis hold the United States to its rhetoric about letting the people decide their own political system, they would probably not pick a federation, let alone a liberal republic. Of course, the Bush administration's rhetoric about democracy and free markets was largely hot air. Local elections were cancelled, the Iraqi press was censored, reconstruction contracts have been given without competition to U.S. companies tied to the Republican Party, and insufficient privatization and marketization of state-controlled industries (especially oil) or other assets have occurred (in fact, there is now desperate talk of saving state-owned industries to retain make-work jobs to keep people from turning to crime and violence against the state). Moreover, even Michael Rubin of the neoconservative American Enterprise Institute has admitted that Iraqis have little control over their own government ministries, over where incoming foreign aid flows, or even over reconstruction of Iraq's electrical infrastructure (despite possessing much local expertise in this area after the first Gulf War).[114]

True self-determination by Iraqis would probably yield a loose confederation of local units, a partition of the country into more than one state, or a combination of confederation and partition. These alternatives have the best chance of reducing the violence and putting Iraqis on the road to peace, stability, and prosperity.

If the United States allows genuine self-determination, the first step would be to withdraw U.S. forces from Iraq. This action would ensure that there was no hint of U.S. coercion to produce a certain political structure. Such a withdrawal would most likely reduce violence in Iraq because the foreign invader and occupier would be gone. Any temporary multinational force would probably be subjected to less violence because it would avoid the perception of being a potentially permanent neocolonial invader and occupier. To some extent, the nascent Iraqi police and security forces might also be less of a target because they would no longer be perceived as lackeys of the imperial superpower.

A Decentralized Government

To reduce the violence even further for the long term, a constitutional convention would have to be held—without the taint of foreign Western intervention and with representatives from each tribe, geographical area, and ethnic and sectarian group. Such self-determination would allow the Iraqis to delineate the local units that would send representatives to the convention. Some in the U.S. government might find this a scary prospect, but even more instability will result—possibly even a civil war among armed groups, as they fight to gain control of a potentially oppressive Iraqi central government—if the Iraqis are denied this possibility, especially after all the U.S. talk about letting Iraqis determine their own future. Instead, some type of decentralized government—a partition, a confederation, or a combination of the two—is the probable outcome of such a convention.

Confederation

A confederation, as mentioned earlier, is somewhere between a federation (for example, the United States or Switzerland) and an alliance or league (for example, the North Atlantic Treaty Organization [NATO]). Unlike a federal government, the government of a confederation does not rule citizens directly, but only indirectly through the governments of component states. A confederation's actions need to be converted into state legislation before they control citizens of the states. If a state fails to implement confederational will, the confederation can sanction only the state and not its citizens. States are much more difficult to coerce than individuals.[115]

Unlike the central government in a federal arrangement, a confederation government is not the strongest level of government in the system—the component states have the greatest power. Confederations resemble treaties among countries.[116] The states do cede control of some limited areas of governance to the confederation government, however, but they keep most areas of governance for themselves. (In most alliances or leagues, countries cooperate but do not cede powers to each other.) The states also usually retain all powers of taxation (and secession). Thus the power lies where control of the money is held.

Confederations Are on the Rise

Until recently, confederations had fallen out of fashion. The perception was that this form of governance was ineffective and that many confederations eventually turned into federations—for example, the United States in the late 1700s[117] and Switzerland in the mid-1800s.[118]

In addition, over time the central government of a federation tends to expand at the expense of the state governments. The United States and Switzerland are again examples of this phenomenon. Over the years, the U.S. Supreme Court, for example, has preferred people over places (that is, states) in its rulings.[119]

Recently, however, there has been talk among experts on federalism that the federation as a form of government may be in decline and that confederations are again on the rise.[120] This paradigm shift may stem from the breakup of Czechoslovakia and the Soviet Union, troubles in the Russian Federation, the spread of secessionist movements, and the coming together of Europe into a confederation.

More generally, the decline of statism and the rise of globalization—as well as the concomitant increase in regionalization—have led to a trend toward creating confederational forms of governance.[121] People want to retain their ethnic identities—sometimes by decentralization and sometimes despite centralization—but at the same time gain the benefits of increased economic linkages with other nations. Thus instead of forming confederations for purposes of security, as in the old days, the new confederations are forming for mainly economic reasons. When based on mutual economic benefit, economic confederations may be much more durable than their older security-driven counterparts, which provided incentives for some states to "free ride" on other states' defense expenditures. (For example, during the American Revolution, some states were reluctant to provide their share of funds for the continental army under George Washington.)

The European Union (EU) is the most visible confederation in the world. Over time, the union has evolved from consultative agreements between nations into a confederational structure. (In only a few very limited areas—on certain economic issues, such as agriculture—the EU acts as a federation, but, in general, it is a confederation.)[122] The EU experiment has spurred similar efforts in other regions of the world. For example, there is also a confederation of Caribbean nations called the Caribbean Community. Great Britain first tried to create a West Indies Federation, but that project failed. Instead, the islands wanted their independence but decided to share a supreme court, the function of higher education, and a currency. The Netherlands formed something similar to a confederation with its former Caribbean colonies when it withdrew from its empire.[123]

The Commonwealth of Independent States, the successor to the Soviet Union, is also a confederation. The EU is a more fully developed confederation than either the Caribbean Community or the Commonwealth of Independent States, but the latter two are moving farther and farther down that path.[124]

Although security considerations drove the origin of the EU and still have some relevance today, the organization is now mainly an economic confederation. It has a common market (tariffs and regulatory nontariff barriers to trade between member states have been removed, and no border controls inhibit the movement of goods, services, or people between member states), a customs union (tariffs on nonmember states' products are uniform), and now a common currency and European central bank. Although the people of various nations are EU citizens and get to vote directly for members of an increasingly powerful European Parliament, few EU citizens migrate from their own state to live and work in another state.[125] More important, the member nations, through the Council of the European Union, still retain the bulk of the governing power (both executive and legislative). In the treaty governing the EU, care was taken to preserve the member nations' sovereignty.

Amendments can be made to the treaty governing the EU only with the "common accord" of the member states and after being ratified by all parties. Individual nations are not bound by amendments and may instead opt to withdraw from the treaty. Unlike in the U.S. Constitution, the treaty does not enumerate the powers of a central government, and EU law does not have supremacy over member nations' laws. The EU's legal system is a series of common modifications to the member nations' legislation rather than a system superior to such national laws. There is no European police force or enforcement agency to enforce EU decisions; member nations' enforcement mechanisms are used instead. Thus, the EU has difficulty making an errant state comply, and member states have the ultimate power to decide what laws will apply in their territories. In sum, the individual member states have the last say, not the EU machinery.[126]

One further indicator that local governments are dominant in the EU is the composition of the European Commission, the EU's executive bureaucracy. Rather than a system in which appointments are made to the commission based on merit or membership in a particular political party, there is an effort to keep a balance of nationalities.[127]

Taxing and spending authority are the ultimate indicators of governmental power. The EU's member states have varying taxation systems and levels of government spending. The EU itself has negligible central taxing power.[128] Also, the EU's budget remains small when compared to those of federations.[129]

There are nascent efforts to derive a common European foreign and defense policy, but most of the all-important security issues are still left to the states, as is the bulk of social and welfare policy. This approach is likely to remain the status quo indefinitely because the EU's supranational "political union" remains only rhetoric.[130]

Thus the EU confederation has exhibited integration mainly in the economic sphere. Although the EU faced secessionist pressures in the late 1970s, it survived because no nation had an interest in withdrawing from the large integrated market. This result illustrates that an economic confederation can be held together by its constituent states' mutual interests, whereas a confederation based only on political or security foundations might prove unstable. In the political or security realm, confederations face a zero-sum game (with gains and losses among the various nations canceling each other out), whereas in the economic sphere, all states win by having a larger market.

Can Confederation Work for Iraq?

Similarly, some sort of an economic confederation might work for Iraq. It would probably handle Iraq's multitude of ethnic, religious, and tribal factions better than a federation would. Of necessity, the confederation's objectives would be more modest than the EU's. Concomitantly, an Iraqi confederation would probably want to avoid a huge central bureaucratic organization like the EU's. But a simple common market and customs union would allow greater economic efficiency and economic growth than separated local markets in the area of a former Iraq. Also, a common currency might allow the continued use of the new Iraqi dinar. All of this commonality might be achieved with little central bureaucracy.

Some analysts, such as Leslie Gelb, former president of the Council on Foreign Relations, and former U.S. ambassador Peter Galbraith have proposed forms of government for Iraq that are weaker than a strong federation. For example, Gelb has proposed a loose federation in which the central government would oversee border defense, the sharing of oil revenues, and health. But this proposal gets the central government into controversial zero-sum issues that are better left to individual regional governments. Galbraith has proposed an even more feasible solution—an even weaker central government, which conducts only foreign affairs and monetary policy, with eventual independence for Kurdistan.[131]

A common foreign and defense policy especially should be avoided. Those who have the guns often use them to control others. For example, the new Iraq-wide army and police raises fears that one faction might get control over these security forces and use them to oppress the other groups. And such fears are well founded. The so-called forces are not really loyal to the national government, but are infested with various ethno-sectarian militias. The United States should disband these Iraq-wide forces before withdrawing. The natural solution to the problem of security is to let the local militias provide security in their own areas.

Or local police forces could be developed or strengthened. As columnist Paul Krugman notes, a weak central authority does not have to mean that terrorists will have a haven in Iraq. For a year after the fall of Saddam Hussein, moderate Shi'i holy men maintained stability and peace in large swaths of Iraq.[132] Also, Kurdish militias have provided excellent security in northern Iraq.

Common social policies should also probably be ruled out. The different tribal, ethnic, and religious groups have their own subcultures, customs, and social organizations. Common social policies would reduce these differences to the lowest common denominator and might very well result in social strife or even civil war. The Kurds, Arab Sunnis, and Shi'a would most likely have different inclinations toward social policy.

The power of taxation should remain at the local level and go no higher—on the principle that people feel they have the most control over and participation in a government that is closest to them rather than a government in some distant capital city. Also, an Iraq confederation might establish a rotating collective presidency—similar to that of Switzerland.[133] Iraq's presidency might have one representative from each local area and have only limited powers.

A confederation, in which component governments are dominant and have autonomy, could even allow different forms of government at the local level—unlike a federation, which requires that the state and federal governments be very similar to each other and to the central government. The EU is a confederation of disparate types of states— for example, Germany is a federation, France is a unitary state, and the United Kingdom is a union.[134] And the expanding European confederation is becoming more diverse in language, history, geography, politics, and wealth.[135] In Iraq, for example, the Shi'a would likely want to have a closer relationship between church and state than would the Kurds. Elazar has argued, moreover, that confederations can handle ethnic tensions better than federations.[136]

Some analysts believe that a true federation requires democratic governments at all levels.[137] Despite the rhetorical flourishes of American politicians, a multilayered liberal democracy is unlikely to develop in

Iraq anytime soon because the political culture for it does not yet exist,[138] and it is unlikely to be successfully superimposed from above by a foreign invader. In fact, in much the same way that free-market capitalism became incorrectly associated with racial apartheid (state-mandated segregation) in South Africa, democracy may very well have become associated in the Middle East with an "infidel" foreign occupation that imposes it at gunpoint. In fact, shortly before the invasion of Iraq (February 26, 2003), a damning classified U.S. State Department report noted that even if a democracy were established in Iraq, the United States was so unpopular that the new democratic Iraqi government would probably be an anti–U.S. Islamic regime.[139]

The government currently running Iraq is largely a strict Islamic regime that is only friendly to the United States because U.S. occupation forces are still in the country. The Iraqi government has good relations with the fundamentalist Islamic regime in Iran.

Liberal democracy has the best chance of success when the political culture for it evolves naturally from the grass roots in a society. History and thirty years of research argue that liberal democracy is also more likely to take root in countries that are more homogeneous and economically developed than Iraq is (for example, postwar Japan or Germany). Saddam's statist economic policies and more than a decade of harsh international economic sanctions and numerous wars have probably made Iraqi society too poor for genuine democracy to blossom anytime soon.[140]

If all local areas in Iraq were allowed to govern themselves the way they wanted, there would be much less potential for conflict. The loose-confederation option does not mean the number of autonomous regions would have to be held to three. The number of autonomous areas would be the result of negotiated Iraqi self-determination. The Kurdish, Sunni, and Shi'i communities are all fragmented and may each generate multiple autonomous areas. In some cases, tribes might govern autonomous regions.

Abba Eban, a former foreign minister of Israel, has noted the conflicting global trends of political fragmentation and economic integration.[141] A post–U.S. Iraq might look like a microcosm of world trends—a confederation that is politically diverse and segmented but economically integrated.

To ensure that local governments have continuing primacy, any new Iraqi confederation might have nullification built into the system. Local governments would be able to nullify any central government legislation that did not fit with local law or customs. (An equivalent would be a requirement for local governments to unanimously approve the confederation's legislation.) In fact, Iraq's Transitional Administrative Law, signed by the Iraqi Governing Council and the U.S. occupation authority in November 2003, contained a form of nullification to benefit the Kurds. The Kurdistan Regional Government could amend Iraqi federal legislation within its jurisdiction. However, the Sunnis and the Shi'i majority, under the leadership of Grand Ayatollah Ali al-Sistani, erased any mention of the law or Kurdish autonomy in the UN Security Council resolution that supported the creation of an Iraqi interim government.[142] Although Kurdish nullification and autonomy are in doubt, the Kurds badly want them and may very well be willing to fight, using their potent militia, if they fail to get them.

Partition

Even with provisions ensuring strong local autonomy, a group (or groups) might not want to be part of any new confederation. To mitigate this potential problem, the option to secede should probably be enshrined in any new Iraqi constitution. Unlike in federations, secession is usually an option in most confederations.[143]

In one recent settlement ending a civil war, the option for eventual secession was written into the agreement. In an attempt to end the brutal and long-running civil war in southern Sudan, an agreement was reached that allowed the black Christian and animist south to have autonomy from the Muslim-dominated Arab government. The decentralized arrangement disperses power to Sudan's constituent states.

Southern Sudan will have its own constitution that will be compatible with that of the interim national constitution. The pact also provides for future referenda on the secession of certain Sudanese regions. The arrangement is not perfect because it does not include all groups or solve all conflicts in Sudan (for example, the conflict in the western region of Darfur), but if such an agreement for decentralization can be reached even amid the internecine hostility of a devastating war has that killed millions, some hope exists that one can be reached in Iraq—a country in which the factions are not yet fighting each other on a grand scale.

The option to secede has the practical effect of preventing the central government from becoming too large and powerful by allowing for exit or the threat of exit. Transactions in a free market work well because the consumer always has the option to exit and buy from someone else; in practice, the exit option does not usually exist vis-à-vis a government unless secession is specifically guaranteed.[144] But if a group insists on seceding—the Kurdish groups among the Iraqi factions are most likely to do so—then the question becomes how that outcome would be handled.

Given that the United States has recklessly destabilized Iraq, however, it must be recognized that a peacefully-arrived-at confederation may not be possible. The fall of the communist bloc illustrates that "democratization" of multi-ethnic countries usually leads to secession and partition—whether peaceful or not.[145]

In the former Yugoslavia, a post–Cold War constitutional confederation on its way to implementation was disposed of in a bloody civil war. The people of the wealthier northern parts of Yugoslavia—Croatians and Slovenians—were more market oriented than the Serbians, who were more statist and who staffed much of the central administration, including the army and secret police.[146] Croatia and Slovenia refused to subsidize the poorer southern regions and seceded unilaterally from them. Serbia, the militarily dominant "republic," challenged their secession, and a bitter internecine war broke out.[147]

The same tragic outcome might very well happen in any Iraqi confederation. After all, Iraq's groups are as fractious as those in Yugoslavia.[148] One way to avoid such a horrific outcome might be an attempt to negotiate any division or confederation in advance, rather than waiting for the unilateral secession of certain regions. Such a successful negotiation resulted in the peaceful partition of Czechoslovakia and the Soviet Union (except in the Caucasus). Also, in Yugoslavia, the seceding republics were, at least initially, militarily inferior to the dominant Serb armed forces. By comparison, in Iraq, each of the groups potentially seceding from the Iraqi government—the Sunnis and Kurds—have equal or greater military power than the majority Shi'i militias, which are split among various competing forces. The Kurdish militia, the strongest of any Iraqi group's forces, is powerful enough that only the U.S. military would be able to prevent their secession attempt.[149] Thus, the Shi'a might be deterred from a replay of Serbia's actions in Yugoslavia—that is, the attempt to keep Iraq together by force of arms. In fact, many of the Shi'a favor autonomy more than the Sunnis, who lack documented oil reserves in their area. But in the wake of targeting by Iraqi government forces infested with Shi'i militias, even the Sunnis have become more receptive to regional autonomy.

Although partitioning Iraq into independent states has some disadvantages, it should be actively considered and may be inevitable. The longer it takes to establish a viable Iraqi central government—if it ever happens at all—the more likely it is that the three regions of Iraq will remain on their diverging trajectories. Some analysts believe that the time has passed when a unified Iraq is possible.[150]

Under partitioning, moving ethnic groups becomes more likely. In some areas of Iraq, the various groups are still mixed, most prominently in and around Baghdad.[151] Some ethnic groups may be "stranded" as minorities in states with majorities from other ethnic groups. If such minorities' rights are not protected, violence may result, as it did in Kosovo between the majority Albanians and the minority Serbs. One alternative is the forced removal of people—usually considered a violation of human rights; another, better solution is to provide incentives for voluntary movement. This problem might be less severe if Iraq were to remain as a loose confederation. The component parts could be smaller than partitioned states and tailored to fit tribal, ethnic, or religious boundary lines. Alternatively, in a partitioned Iraq, minority rights might be guaranteed by deterrence. Country A's government would be deterred from harming members of country B's ethnic/religious group within A's borders by the threat that country B would do the same to members of A's group within B's borders, and vice versa. Thus both governments might be deterred from persecuting minorities.[152]

Effect of a Partitioned Iraq on Neighboring States

Another potential problem with an outright partition is that neighboring states may feel more threatened by or take advantage of a partitioned Iraq. But these fears may be overstated. Some analysts argue that if Iraqi Kurdistan became a separate state or states, Turkey would invade, fearing that its own Kurdish minority would get ideas of separating from Turkey and perhaps merging with the new Kurdish state(s).

Despite Turkey's blustering over the issue and armed incursions into Kurdish Iraq, however, it has lived with de facto Kurdish self-rule in northern Iraq for more than a decade. The Turks have much investment in Iraqi Kurdistan, which would be endangered by any Turkish attack on the region. Also, the Turks desperately want to become members of the EU, and any belligerent action against the Iraqi Kurds would nix that possibility. The desire for EU membership may be a significant reason as to why the Turks have recently been more accommodating to the Iraqi Kurdish government. And if Turkey gets EU membership—which would bring economic benefits but also demand that member states recognize minority languages and cultures—Turkish Kurds might be less likely to favor independence. By staying with Turkey in the EU, the Turkish Kurds would be wealthier than their Iraqi brethren. The voting patterns of Turkish Kurds already indicate that a majority does not favor separation from Turkey.[153] These realities should make Turkey less nervous about a new Kurdish state on its borders.

Furthermore, if the Iraqi Kurds give up any attempt to absorb Kirkuk—a city containing many Turkmen and nearby oil reserves—and respect Turkmen minority rights, Turkey might acquiesce to independence for Iraqi Kurdistan rather than quash it with force. If Turkey had to choose between a dysfunctional Islamist and unified Iraq and a Kurdish rump state as its neighbor, it might very well choose the latter.[154]

Although the Iraqi Kurds should have the right of self-determination and would probably prefer a separate state or states, perhaps any possibility of a Turkish invasion would moderate their push to secede from Iraq and cause them to accept a confederation. (Even if it did not, a landlocked, independent Iraqi Kurdistan would need friendly relations with Turkey to help keep open links to the world.) Thus the Turks might very well tolerate formal recognition of the current actuality in Kurdistan—Kurdish autonomy. Chatham House noted that "the common expectation that Turkey will immediately intervene militarily if the fragmentation scenario prevails is overdrawn."[155]

Some argue that other neighboring nations, rather than being threatened by a decentralized Iraq, would take advantage of the situation.[156] For example, they argue that Shi'i Iran would have undue influence over Iraqi Shi'a or would want to form some sort of a political arrangement with them. But the Iraqi Shi'a are Arabs, whereas the Iranian Shi'a are Persians, thus having different cultures. More important, it is more likely that the Iraqi Shi'a would influence the Iranian Shi'a rather than vice versa. The cradle of the Shi'i sect of Islam is in Iraq, not in Iran. The post-Saddam opening of the holiest Shi'i shrines in Najaf and Karbala to Shi'a from around the world and the greater stature of Iraq's Grand Ayatollah Ali al-Sistani, compared to any religious leader in Iran, might force the Iranian Shi'a to play second fiddle to their Iraqi counterparts.

Also, the Iraqi Shi'a have a more moderate view about church-state relations than do the hard-line clerics in Tehran. In fact, the Iraqi clerics in Najaf regard the Iranian ayatollahs' involvement in the government there as running counter to Shi'i Islam.[157] Additionally, the main goal of the Iranian religious conservatives is to have Shi'i majority control of a central government that governs all of Iraq.[158] A very decentralized Iraq, run at the local level, would effectively deny the Iranians this objective.

The Israeli government's first choice would be a unified democratic Iraq under continued U.S. tutelage. As noted previously, however, the Israelis seem to have written that possibility off as early as August 2003. As a fallback position, they would prefer a less threatening, decentralized Iraq to a unified Iraq with a strict Shi'i Islamic government. They have already gained influence in Iraqi Kurdistan training the Kurdish militias, which want to maintain the autonomy of Iraqi Kurdistan from the central government and may even want eventual independence. Therefore, various countries, not just those hostile to the United States, would be gaining influence in a fragmented Iraq.

Can the States of a Partitioned Iraq Survive?

There is a fear that the smaller states of a partitioned Iraq would be unable to defend themselves against their larger neighbors. As the Israeli support of the Kurds shows, however, the smaller states would undoubtedly have the help of outside powers with interests in the region. In addition, small states everywhere, including those in the Persian Gulf (for example, Qatar, Bahrain, and the United Arab Emirates), have had to make accommodations—some have made them very skillfully—with larger nations to assure their security. The new states of the former Iraq would have to learn how to conduct such statecraft. (Besides, the world survived Iraq's being diminished by numerous wars and by more than a decade of crushing international economic sanctions, thus allowing it to act only as a weakened counterweight to Iran; it can probably survive three or more ministates in Iraq's place.)

Economically, there is no minimum size for a newly independent area to be viable, especially if it allows cultural interaction and free trade and financial flows with other states in the region and the world.

In response to another concern, partition does not have to create a haven for "terrorists." Iraq has militias that can maintain security. Quite the contrary, if partition achieved its goal of enhanced stability, compared to the current instability, havens for terrorism would be reduced. And if the United States removes its forces from Iraqi territory, any terrorists who do hole up in one of the new states would be much less likely to attack the United States. If there is any doubt that less U.S. military intervention in the Islamic world would reduce anti–U.S. blowback terrorism, the example of U.S. intervention in Lebanon during the 1980s is instructive. After the United States withdrew its military forces from Lebanon, attacks on U.S. targets by the Shi'i Lebanese-based Hezbollah group eventually evaporated. Furthermore, some Sunnis are now reacting to the bloody excesses of al Qaeda by fighting the group. Other Sunnis tolerate al Qaeda only because the group fights the foreign occupiers; once the U.S. is gone, they would probably also turn on the group.

Overly Skeptical of Partition, Critics Overlook Success Stories

Critics of partitioning Iraq, including much of the Bush administration and the international community, maintained that dividing countries is dangerous.[159] The critics pointed to the past bloody partitions of Northern Ireland, Palestine, and the Indian subcontinent as evidence. The critics are, of course, correct that partitioning countries has risks, but rarely do they present a viable alternative to partitioning Iraq— especially when a de facto armed partition already exists and ethno-sectarian cleavages have been shown to impair national reconciliation so as to make a viable unified democratic government impossible. In some past cases, partition failed because the ethnic conflict was so great that all else had failed and partition was tried as a last resort to a very tough problem. In Iraq, partition could be tried as a last-ditch effort to save the country from exploding in a full-blown civil war. The longer the wait to partition, however, the less likely it is to succeed. The Shi'a have split into warring factions, as have the Sunnis, and the Kurds have always had two factions. Iraq is turning into a Somalia-like patchwork of armed ethno-sectarian and tribal city-states. As factions split and more groups are formed, overall agreement on a partitioning arrangement gets more difficult.

As for their analysis of the three failed cases of Northern Ireland, Palestine, and British India, the critics are wrong. The concept of partitioning was not to blame for the violence in these three well-known cases, but instead it was the disastrous ways these particular partitions were carried out—especially the way that boundaries were drawn. As Chaim Kaufmann, a professor of international relations at Lehigh University, pointed out, even in these three disastrous cases, separating populations reduced most violence; continued strife in certain specific local areas actually resulted from the incomplete quarantining of the warring sides. Another example of an incomplete partition causing continued violence was seen during the secession of Croatia and Bosnia from Yugoslavia in 1991 and 1992.[160]

The critics also ignore partitions that were successful at preventing further violence, such as that of Outer Mongolia from China (1921), Taiwan from China (1950), Bangladesh from Pakistan (1971), Cyprus (1974), and eventually Bosnia (after the Dayton Agreement in 1995). And they conveniently overlook peaceful partitions, such as Hungary from the Austro-Hungarian Empire (1867), Norway from Sweden (1905), Senegal and Soudan (Mali) from the Mali Federation, Jamaica from the Federation of the West Indies (1961), Singapore from Malaysia (1965), Czechoslovakia (1993), and most of the former Soviet Union (1991). (Exceptions include the Soviet use of force in what turned out to be a futile attempt to stop Lithuanian and Georgian independence[161] and Azeri nationalists, who were fighting Armenian nationalists over the fate of the Nagorno Karabakh province in Azerbaijan.)[162]

Critics Promote Inferior Alternatives to Partition

Generally, critics of partition rarely come up with a better practical alternative. Other more "politically correct" options are often worse than partition. On the basis of his case studies of partition, Kaufmann perceptively concluded:

Solutions that aim both to restore multi-ethnic civil politics and to avoid population transfers, such as institution building, power sharing, and identity reconstruction, cannot work during or after an ethnic civil war because they do not resolve the security dilemma created by mixed demography. As long as both sides know that the best security strategy for each is to engage in offense and in ethnic cleansing, neither can entrust its security to hope for the other's restraint. The policy implication is that the international community should endorse separation as a remedy for at least some communal conflicts; otherwise, the processes of war will separate the populations anyway, at much higher human cost.[163]

Once again, a federation is a system in which a fairly powerful central government rules citizens directly, but nevertheless shares some power with regional governments. In a federation, however, Robert Dorff, an expert on federalism, notes that success at societal conflict management depends not just on government structure, but on having a cooperative political culture among governments.[164] Daniel J. Elazar put it best:

Elements of a federal process include a sense of partnership on the part of the parties to the federal compact, manifested through negotiated cooperation on issues and programs and based on a commitment to open bargaining between all parties to an issue in such a way as to strive for consensus or, failing that, an accommodation which protects the fundamental integrity of all partners.[165]

Similarly, Uri Ra'anan, Maria Mesner, Keith Armes, and Kate Martin assert that

Any solutions to the problems of multi-ethnic states along such [federal] lines depend critically on the various groups' willingness to accept rational, compromise solutions, to give up claims to territorial autonomy, and to trust the state administration to respect and protect the cultural rights of diverse groups in an evenhanded way.[166]

In a review of Ra'anan, Mesner, Armes, and Martin's book, Gary B. Cohen notes that, "Such favorable conditions have been rare indeed during . . . more than eight decades."[167]

Unfortunately, Iraq, with its ethno-sectarian fissures, does not have the cooperative political culture for a federation to be viable. The proper political culture must be in place before federal institutions are likely to succeed.[168] Therefore, such institutions cannot be imposed from above—especially by an outside power at gunpoint—and be expected to be embraced by the populace and to flourish. Moreover, ethno-sectarian groups in Iraq—especially the Kurds and Shi'a, and increasingly the Sunnis—do not want to give up territorial autonomy, and they distrust that a strong central government will not be used by one group to repress the others. These obvious facts escaped the Bush administration before its catastrophic attempt to invade and "democratize" a unified Iraq.

Consociationalism is a system in which ethno-religious groups share power in the central government and in which each group has a veto over the policies of that government—for example, the central government in Bosnia and Herzegovina following the Dayton Agreement. In contrast to a federation—consociational or otherwise—in a more decentralized confederation, the central government cannot rule the populace directly, but must go through the regional governments.[169] The latter could be drawn along ethno-sectarian lines. Thus decentralized confederations require less societal cooperation to function successfully than federations or even consociational governing arrangements.

In a laudable attempt to end Sudan's long-running civil war, which killed millions of people, as mentioned earlier, the Arab-dominated Islamic government and the black, Christian, and animist rebels in the southern part of the country reached an agreement in 2005 to decentralize and maybe eventually partition the country. The agreement was for the south to get autonomy from the central government, and, unfortunately, for the two groups to share power by combining their organizations in a national unity government until multiparty elections are held in 2009. The agreement also provided for a referendum in 2011 for southerners to decide whether to remain in Sudan or become an independent country.[170]

The principal problem with the agreement has turned out to be its attempt to integrate the central government, while decentralizing—and maybe eventually dividing—the country. The consociational power-sharing agreement for the central government has proved unstable and has avoided the major issue of where to draw the border between the north and the south—where many of Sudan's oil reserves lie. In retrospect, it probably would have been better to avoid the power-sharing arrangement and to just focus on autonomy for the south with the eventual option of partition. The time spent on agreeing to power sharing should have been used on negotiating the route of the border to ensure an equitable sharing of oil fields between north and south.

Regrettably, the international community also continues to adhere to such politically correct multi-ethnic solutions and has an aversion to even voluntary population transfers for the separation of groups—even when groups exhibit vitriolic hostility toward one another and don't want to live together. Sovereign states in the international community naturally place state sovereignty above self-determination, which often can be a danger to them.[171] After violence is reduced in a particular conflict, a tendency exists to attempt to resettle refugees in their previous neighborhoods. For example, in Iraq, the attenuated violence in 2007 has led to ill-advised Iraqi government attempts to encourage the return of refugees of one ethno-sectarian group to their homes in an area now dominated by another such group. Although the refugees have a right to do so, such returns en masse might very well lead to another round of violent ethnic cleansing. Similarly, the U.S. and Iraqi governments sending security forces made up of one ethno-sectarian group to police areas dominated by another group in order to cultivate the forces' "national identification" has been folly. Because most Iraqis owe primary allegiance to their ethno-sectarian group, not the Iraqi state or government, this policy has only caused resentment and violence.[172]

Instead, the global community needs to reject such politically correct multi-ethno-sectarian solutions and pay more attention to the growing body of academic literature arguing that partitions of states on an ethno-sectarian basis can reduce violence among warring groups within that state. In other words, the old cliché "good fences make good neighbors" turns out to be true.

The Best Way Out: Self-Determination and Decentralization

Permitting Iraq to have self-determination—and likely a decentralized form of governance, or even complete partition—is not a perfect solution, but it is very probably the best way out of what has become an ill-advised military adventure. This policy alternative would allow the United States to act more in accordance with its founding principles, cut its losses in credibility from an unnecessary invasion and occupation, escape a nasty quagmire, remove a huge financial albatross hanging from taxpayers' necks, and say that it removed a dictator and gave Iraq the best chance for future peace and prosperity. Today, there is much hand-wringing among the U.S. foreign elite about what to do in another half-hearted Vietnam-like war. The exit strategy proposed here is the best and only real option.

4 | Implementation

IN MANY RESPECTS, Iraq has already been divided. The Kurds have had their own semiautonomous region since the first Persian Gulf War ended in 1991. The current Iraqi Constitution permits the creation of powerful regions, and some Shi'i Arab leaders have talked about creating a Shi'i autonomous region in southern Iraq. Even the Sunni Arabs—long the Iraqi group most opposed to decentralization because few oil reserves have been confirmed in their region in central Iraq—have begun to talk about threatening to secede from the nation. Local militias or guerrillas—based on ethnic, sectarian, or tribal allegiances—already provide security in many parts of the country.

Whether the Bush administration admitted it or not, the policies of its chief on-scene commander in Iraq, General David Petraeus, implicitly gave up on creating a unified democratic Iraq and recognized that stability required an acknowledgment of the fragmented reality on the ground. The United States has always supported the Kurdish Peshmerga militias. At the same time, Petraeus continued to train Iraqi security forces, which are heavily infested with Shi'i militias. Petraeus did not challenge the Supreme Islamic Iraqi Council, which controlled most towns in the Shi'i south. Also, he did not pursue the militant Shi'i militia of Moqtada al-Sadr, but instead actually aided al-Sadr by working with his group to provide aid and services in certain Shi'i areas and by pursuing only more radical renegade factions of that militia. Finally, Petraeus effectively deputized—by subsidizing, arming, and training—former Sunni guerrillas (the Sunni Awakening Movement) to police

Sunni areas and fight al Qaeda.[173] Yet there is potentially explosive resistance from the Shi'i government to integrating these Sunni fighters into the mostly Shi'i security forces. The Shi'i government has even tried to arrest many leaders of the Awakening Movement. Thus, once the overstretched U.S. military is compelled to draw down forces from its troop surge and U.S. subsidies to the Sunnis inevitably dissipate, sectarian militias and guerillas, which have been lying low, will probably again escalate violence. The United States will likely have trained and armed most of the factions in a multisided civil war.

Even worse, a state of de facto and unratified partition is probably the most dangerous situation for Iraq. Petraeus tried to achieve short-term stability—to buy time for national reconciliation—but he actually implicitly reinforced the country's existing partition. And, as mentioned earlier, with the fractured nature of Iraqi society, true national reconciliation is unlikely to occur.

The existing de facto partition is unratified by the various ethno-sectarian and tribal groups because brute force of arms—that is, ethnic cleansing—created it rather than negotiation and agreement. Without an agreement among groups at a national conclave on the boundaries of new autonomous ethno-sectarian or tribal regions (or independent states) and a subsequent voluntary movement of peoples to achieve more homogeneous political units, an all-out, multisided civil war will probably result over disputed territory and from the fears of large minorities caught on the wrong side of the dividing lines. Thus Iraq's already-existing partition has to be adjusted and the new boundaries ratified by all ethno-sectarian or tribal groups, preferably in the form of a loose confederation of autonomous regions.

Fifteen Lessons from Previous Partitions

This book primarily examines the historical record of ethno-sectarian partition and secession mainly during the twentieth and twenty-first centuries. Although the history of partition and secession goes back to the ancient world, those divisions were not based on ethno-sectarian self-determination. For the most part, the concept of self-determination became influential in world affairs only at the beginning of the twentieth century. Prior to the twentieth century, most of the globe outside Europe and the Americas was subjected to colonial rule.[174]

Important lessons can be learned from the history of partition and secession during the twentieth and twenty-first centuries. In many cases, more can be learned from failed partitions than from successful ones. The fifteen lessons are as follows:

1. Ethno-sectarian aspirations can rise again after years of being suppressed.
2. An outside power cannot impose a sustainable partition.
3. All parties must agree to partition.
4. Boundaries between regions should be set to avoid stranding large minorities on the "wrong" side.
5. Boundaries should also consider resources and cultural and religious sites.
6. Regions should be defensible but don't necessarily have to be contiguous.
7. Population movements may be necessary, but they must be voluntary.
8. Adequate security must be provided for population movements.
9. A decentralized Iraq does not need to have only three autonomous regions.
10. If any central government remains, it must be weak.
11. Peacefully negotiated partitions reduce international conflict.
12. Powerful neighbors must be brought into the partition process.
13. Regions may each have a different form of government.
14. An international peacekeeping force may be needed for a time after partition.
15. Caution: autonomous regions may eventually turn into independent states.

1. *Ethno-Sectarian Aspirations Can Rise Again After Years of Being Suppressed*

After World War II, national self-determination became a major force in the international system. At first, colonial possessions wanted independence from their imperial masters. Later, even rich, stable countries have experienced secessionist sentiments—for example, the Quebeçois in Canada, the Scots in the United Kingdom, and the Flemish in Belgium. Recently, Belgium was not able to form a government for a long period and might very well eventually break up. As with the Czechs in Czechoslovakia, the now richer Dutch-speaking Flemish are balking at continuing to subsidize the poorer French-speaking Walloons.[175] Regional and global economic integration, which increase the economic viability and security of small states, have assisted in this push for ethno-sectarian self-determination.

As a result of these many movements for self-determination, there are now almost two hundred nation-states in the world. Over time, the nationalist movements have become narrower and narrower—for example, Yugoslav nationalism turned into Croatian, Slovenian, and Serbian nationalism.[176] Now Iraqi nationalism vis-à-vis the British has turned into a movement toward Shi'i, Kurd, and even Sunni nationalism.

In Iraq, it is said that the Shi'i and Sunni groups lived in peace and intermingled under Saddam Hussein—implying that they could do it again in post-Saddam Iraq. But that peace was enforced with brutal authoritarianism; Saddam and other post–World War II Sunni strongmen brutally quashed Shi'i and Kurdish uprisings during their tenure. Some of these episodes of violence were just more installments of the conflict existing in the Islamic world between Sunnis and Shi'a since the prophet Muhammad's death in 632 CE. The country's ethno-sectarian identities were suppressed under many Sunni kings and dictators, including Saddam, but have now resurfaced with the end of authoritarianism. Without a return to autocracy, it is unlikely that these genies can be put back into the bottle.

Such rekindling of smoldering ethno-sectarian identities, after a long period of repression, has occurred before. Examples abound of ethno-sectarian identification reigniting after long periods of being subsumed into larger states and empires. Although not exhibiting nationalism in the modern sense, ancient cities reasserted themselves after the great powers of the Sargonid Empire, Sparta, Thebes, and Macedonia tried unsuccessfully to permanently absorb them.[177]

In 1815, the victors of the Napoleonic Wars wiped Poland off the map as an independent country. This was the second time an independent Poland had been terminated. Starting in 1772, Poland underwent three partitions, each time losing territory until it became extinct in 1796 when Prussia, Austria, and Russia devoured it. Napoleon revived it in 1807, but the nations ultimately victorious against him retired Poland again at the Congress of Vienna in 1815—with Russia governing the remnant and later incorporating it.[178] This erasure lasted for more than a hundred years until the allies in World War I carved a new Poland out of Germany, Austria, and Russia—states that were weakened in the war.[179] After the Nazis and Soviets divided Poland again in 1939, it was yet again reborn in 1945.[180] Polish history shows how resilient nationalist sentiments can be.

As a result of the revolutions that spread like wildfire across Europe in 1848, Hungary declared its independence from the Austro-Hungarian Empire in April 1849. The Russians crushed the revolt and returned Hungary to the Austrian emperor. In an effort to gain more autonomy, the Hungarians boycotted this national government. Hungary's quest for autonomy was not achieved until Austria and Hungary separated in 1867. Thus the Austro-Hungarian Empire's partition was achieved peacefully.

The Hungarian constitution and government was restored, Austrian Emperor Franz Joseph became the king of Hungary, and a confederation was formed that had a small number of joint ministries, common budgets to fund them, and common tariffs within the empire. Such a weak central government and a limited confederation—focused on maintaining a free trade area and establishing regional autonomy on policies toward minorities and religion[181]—might be a model for modern-day Iraq. In fact, in Iraq, given the ethnic strife among ethno-sectarian groups competing for control of the central government, that government may have to be even weaker than in the Austro-Hungarian case.

Several southern European Slavic groups, previously in different countries and empires, were united into a created Yugoslavia after World War I. The communists, who governed the federal structure instituted after World War II, repressed the nationalism of these various groups.[182] For example, even though communist ruler Josip Broz Tito was part Croatian, he suppressed Croatian nationalism. The Serbs, on the winning Allied side in World War I and thus dominant in Yugoslavia in the interwar period, felt cheated territorially by the post–World War II federal structure. This perception eventually led to inflamed Serb nationalism and efforts to absorb other previously autonomous areas (Montenegro, Vojvodina, and Kosovo) into a greater Serbia.[183] These actions led to a nationalist reaction from the other ethno-religious groups in Yugoslavia.[184] After the communist system fell, these various nationalisms reignited, and Yugoslavia disintegrated via wars over secession in various constituent republics. Leaving significant ethno-sectarian minorities on the other side of the new boundary lines caused these wars.

Even within Serbia, national separatism was rekindled. Kosovo, a province of Serbia with an Albanian majority, attained autonomy in the 1960s. The area lost this status in 1989 and was subjected to a Serb military occupation. This revocation of autonomy—always more dangerous than not granting that status in the first place—eventually led to the Albanian Kosovars going to war for secession and winning it in 1999. Thus, it is tough for a central government, having given regional autonomy, to take it back—even with armed force. In Iraq, the central government is now having a similar tug-of-war with the Kurds, who have had autonomy since the end of the first Gulf War in 1991. The central government would like to reduce Kurdish autonomy somewhat, especially with regard to control over oil reserves. This outcome is unlikely without much bloodshed and even then may not be successful.

Another example of resurfaced nationalism is in the Baltics. As a result of the Nazi-Soviet Pact of 1939, the Soviet Union coercively assimilated the small Baltic republics of Latvia, Lithuania, and Estonia.[185] When the Soviet Union collapsed more than fifty years later, these states again wanted their independence.

In 1814, Norway—for centuries an independent kingdom and subsequently a Danish (or Swedish) possession[186]—was given to Sweden, then under the rule of Swedish King Charles XIII. Norwegians objected to this transfer from Denmark to Sweden. Norway's latent nationalism— buried for centuries—resurfaced ninety years after its transfer to Sweden, resisted deeper political union, and demanded to be free of Swedish control of Norwegian commerce abroad. This dispute over Norwegian commercial policy almost provoked a war with Sweden in 1895. In 1905, the Norwegian parliament dissolved the union with Sweden.[187] Long-dormant Norwegian nationalism had risen again and triumphed.

Singapore seceded peacefully from Malaysia after being a part of that country for only two years. The federation of Malaysia was contrived in 1963 to facilitate British withdrawal from their colonial presence. Since the 1800s, during the colonial era, the British had governed the colonies of Singapore and the Malay states as a unified economic entity (using a common currency since 1906), and the British had led defense cooperation between the two colonies since 1951.

The biggest issue was ethnic identity. Entry into the federation of a Singaporean population that was 80 percent Chinese threatened the special status of Malays, who became a minority. The Singaporean leader's push for equality of individuals threatened the traditional communitarian accommodation between the elites of various racial groups. Even before the race riots of 1965 in Singapore, the Malaysian prime minister decided that it was time for Singapore to leave the federation.[188]

Prior to World War II, Eritrea was an Italian colony, but Italy's defeat in that war threw its status into limbo. In 1950, without allowing Eritreans to have a say, the United Nations imposed, at U.S. urging, a U.S.–style federation on Eritrea and Ethiopia in which the federal government was the Ethiopian crown. Wanting to obtain access to the sea, landlocked Ethiopia first used military force to suppress Eritrea's autonomy under the federation and then, in 1962, forcibly annexed the area.[189] In 1993, Eritrea held a referendum on secession and then seceded.[190] Yet a war broke out later between the two countries over borders that were poorly drawn. As will be discussed later, drawing sustainable borders is the key to any successful partition.

Even gifted leaders usually cannot hold together areas of different history, culture, language, and ethnicity, especially when they have been combined by an outside power into an artificial state with a fairly short history. The previous examples have shown that communal sentiments can resurface long after being submerged. In the cases of Pakistan in 1947 and present-day Iraq, those ethno-sectarian feelings have had a much shorter time to be artificially repressed. And even comparing the cases of Pakistan and Iraq, Iraq's turmoil is occurring at a time when such "nationalisms" have become more and more narrow as post–World War II history has unfolded. Iraq is already partitioned on the ground, and odds are that this reality will eventually have to be acknowledged formally.

2. An Outside Power Cannot Impose a Sustainable Partition

The history of past partitions indicates this lesson—that an outside power cannot impose a sustainable partition—may be the most important in this paper. Partitions perceived as being dictated by outside powers are often prone to disaster. In other words, in Iraq, the United States should not force-feed the recommendations in this paper. There has been enough of this top-down intervention already.

Britain partitioned Ireland in 1921 and the Indian subcontinent in 1947, and allowed the partition of Palestine in 1948; all ended in violence, in part because the locals saw the partitions as the illegitimate work of an outside power. When Ireland was partitioned between the north and south, instead of allowing the Irish to do the dividing themselves, the British parliament did it. The Protestants in the northern part of the Emerald Isle, having much clout in that legislative body, wanted the maximum amount of territory possible and had the boundary of Protestant-dominated Northern Ireland drawn too far south. Leaving a substantial minority of Catholics north of the boundary line resulted in many decades of violence between Protestants and Catholics, which has only subsided recently.

In 1947, although the British took input from the Muslims, Hindus, and Sikhs before partitioning the Indian subcontinent, a British judge came to India, stayed only six weeks, and chaired boundary commissions that drew 3,800 miles of borders between Muslim East and West Pakistan and Hindu India on a map using outdated and likely inaccurate census data. The judge never traveled to see where the border would actually run.[191] The British top-down-driven partition plan, which the local populations perceived as illegitimate, ignored the realities on the ground. Communities were cut off from sites of religious pilgrimage, factories were split from their raw materials, and railways and forests were split in half.

The partition created one of the worst humanitarian disasters of the twentieth century (five hundred thousand to one million died and twelve million people migrated) because it was done too rapidly and in a deliberately vague manner. No one knew whether citizenship in the two new states was based on religion or on universal right, whether people were expected to move to the state where their coreligionists were in the majority, or where the exact borders were to be drawn. The British viceroy, Lord Mountbatten, strangely kept the actual boundaries of the new states a secret until after the official day of partition, thus causing much uncertainty. All of these unanswered questions, and the fears they produced, resulted in massive violence.[192]

Because of a Jewish rebellion, Britain allowed the Jews to provocatively ethnically cleanse Arabs from parts of Palestine and to declare Israeli statehood—something the Arabs perceived as an external power giving land to a neocolonial group of outsiders—land which the British had already promised to the Arabs (as a reward for fighting the Ottoman Turks in World War I). The United States and the United Nations also helped impose this partition on the unwilling Arabs, who made up the vast majority of the population in Palestine. Although large numbers of Arabs were expelled from the Jewish state, a substantial Arabic population has remained within its borders. Also, after the 1967 war, Jews were allowed to settle in the occupied West Bank and Gaza—further intertwining the Jewish and Arabic populations. For decades since, endemic violence has been the result.

In Iraq, the United States should heed the lessons of the past and allow the Iraqis to formulate and implement any partition they choose. The legitimacy of the U.S. occupation is now so weak that the United States might want to stay out of any national conclave among Iraqi groups on decentralization. The U.S. government might act only as a behind-the-scenes counselor, offering suggestions and incentives but allowing the Iraqis to make their own decisions and then implement them. Any coerced partition would likely fail due to a lack of legitimacy. Thus the dos and don'ts in this paper should be taken as suggestions to the Iraqis based on past history, instead of being regarded as demands by an outside power.

The United States does, however, need to act in its own interests and could provide incentives for the Iraqis to reach an agreement ratifying its existing de facto partition. The United States should declare its intention to rapidly withdraw all of its troops from Iraq—removing the final pillar from the dysfunctional and corrupt Iraqi government—therefore forcing the ruling Shi'a and Kurds to negotiate with the Sunnis over partitioning the country. The Sunnis are the most reluctant to ratify such an arrangement because they don't have many documented oil reserves in their territory. But they seem to be coming around, as is the entire Iraqi population. To avoid a full-blown civil war after a U.S. troop withdrawal, the Shi'a and Kurds would likely have an incentive to reach an oil-sharing agreement with the Sunnis as part of an overall partition arrangement.

3. All Parties Must Agree to Partition

The importance of bringing the Sunnis on board the partition train cannot be overstated. Past partitions indicate that if all political groups don't agree to a division prior to a split, then violence will result. In Palestine, the Arabs, who made up the vast majority of the population there, did not agree to the partition and threatened war if it occurred. That problem did not dissuade President Harry S Truman from supporting and lobbying in the United Nations for Israeli statehood, the Jews from declaring it, and Truman—behind in the polls in his 1948 election bid and searching for every vote—from recognizing the new state just eleven minutes after it was declared. The Jews, the British, the United States, and a majority of the nations of the United Nations imposed a partition on the unwilling Arabs.[193] Cutting a deal with the Arabs in advance might have prevented decades of war, even if the Jews would have had to make significant territorial concessions. As can be seen today, this "land for peace" swap is hard to hammer out in practice. But such a deal might have been easier to attain back then before decades of animosity festered.

The creation of Poland is another example of all peoples in a region not agreeing to a partition—with years of war the result. In 1918, the victors of World War I re-created Poland after it had lost its independence over a hundred years earlier. Poland was created from the territories of Germany, Austria, Soviet Russia, Lithuania, and Ukraine. It used military force against the latter three countries to fight over land. After Poland's reemergence, one-third of the people within its borders had no Polish ethnicity and did not speak Polish.[194] This large minority of non-Poles in the new Poland caused major problems (see lesson number four below). Neighbors disputing this outcome led to further trouble. In 1939, Nazi Germany invaded Poland, and the Nazis and Soviets, in the Ribbentrop-Molotov Pact, partitioned the country yet again.

Similarly, much of the violence during the partition of the Indian subcontinent was caused by the fact that the well-armed minority Sikh population did not want to live under Muslim rule. When the British drew the partition line, not enough was done to accommodate Sikh self-determination. Although Britain got agreement from Muslims and Hindus for a partition, the Sikhs decided to fight because they did not want to be included in Pakistan, but instead wanted a Sikh homeland—either as an independent state or as part of India. The incomplete partition agreement did not provide for such a homeland. The leaders of various groups in South Asia agreed to the partition, but it was sprung rapidly on the general population in a vague and deceptive manner. The plan had little popular legitimacy because it had not been debated.[195]

So in Iraq, for partition to work, all factions and at least most of their followers must agree to it or the effort will be worse than futile. As noted earlier, a de facto partition in Iraq already exists and only the boundaries need to be adjusted and ratified by the groups. The Iraqi groups seem to realize that none of them is strong enough to conquer and govern all of Iraq. To avoid a full-blown civil war, all groups have an incentive to reach a partition agreement.

Yet as in the intractable conflict in Palestine, the passions may run too deep in Iraq to get the parties to agree to a "rational" settlement suggested by "experts"—that is, consensus on regional borders and rules for governing a loose confederation (or an outright division of the country). Unlike Palestine, however, Iraq has had fewer years of internecine violence, and thus Iraqi groups may be less bitter toward each other than the Israelis and Palestinians have been. Nevertheless, if the Iraqi groups cannot arrive at a partition agreement even with the shadow of an imminent U.S. withdrawal providing ample incentives, then that is an important signal that a civil war is almost inevitable. The United States could then at last leave Iraq knowing it could do nothing more to prevent such an outcome.

4. *Boundaries Between Regions Should Be Set to Avoid Stranding Large Minorities on the "Wrong" Side*

Critics of partitioning Iraq into autonomous regions or separate states argue that population intermingling in the major cities would prevent a perfect partition of the country. Unfortunately, however, prior ethnic cleansing in many cities has made potential partitioning easier by creating more homogeneous areas. For example, as much as 70 percent of Baghdad is segregated on a sectarian basis;[196] the city now has a Shi'i eastern sector and a Sunni western sector. Although the recent drop in violence in Iraq has been attributed to the surge of thirty thousand added U.S. troops, the same elevated level of forces occurred in 2005 but violence actually increased. Many analysts, including those in the U.S. government, think that the ethnic separation in Baghdad has had more effect on ameliorating the carnage than any astuteness in U.S. counter-insurgency strategy.[197]

More important, history shows that partitions don't need to be perfect to work and the commonsense notion that separating hostile populations would likely prevent future violence is valid. Even in 1861, much before the rise of nationalist movements for self-determination, John Stuart Mill realized that, "Free institutions are next to impossible in a country made up of different nationalities. . . . It is in general a necessary condition for free institutions that the boundaries of government should coincide *in the main* with those of nationalities" (my emphasis).[198]

For an effective ("virtually complete") partition, it is not necessary to ensure that every member of an ethno-sectarian group is on that faction's side of a dividing line. As long as only a small minority is on the other side, it will not threaten the majority population. Only when larger minorities are trapped on the other side of a line, which this paper terms an "incomplete partition," does a security dilemma arise. According to research by Professor Jaroslav Tir, Department of International

Affairs, University of Georgia, this problem often occurs when the old internal administrative boundaries of an original state are used to create the new borders for new autonomous regions or successor states. Such a division has been tried many times, but should be avoided in the future. In fact, Tir concludes that ethnically related border disputes are more prone to cause violence than those involving strategic or economic issues (for example, oil), and thus advises boundary makers to get rid of ethnic disputes even if they cause strategic and economic issues to arise.[199]

Here's why ethnic boundaries can be so inflammatory. When large ethno-sectarian minorities are trapped on the other side of a boundary line, any move by the substantial minority or the majority to arm itself in self-defense will dangerously threaten the other group. Furthermore, intermingling between a majority and a large minority will increase the risk of this offensive threat. In addition, a threatened group may attempt to discriminate against, restrict, disenfranchise, expel, or eradicate members of the other group.[200] In contrast, when the minority on the other side of a line is small enough, the majority is not threatened by it and there is less chance that violence will occur.

The contrast between an incomplete partition and a virtually complete one is illustrated by the vastly different outcomes in the breakups of Yugoslavia in 1991 and 1992 and Czechoslovakia in 1993, respectively.

In June 1991, in the multi-ethnic state of Yugoslavia, Slovenia and Croatia declared independence, with subsequent declarations by Bosnia and Herzegovina and by Macedonia. In September 1991, the majority Albanians in Kosovo, a province in Serbia, declared their independence from the Serbs. In December 1991, the substantial Serb minority in Croatia declared the independent Serbian Republic of Krajina. In March 1992, the significant Serb minority in Bosnia and Herzegovina declared the Republic of Srpska. In April 1992, Serbia and Montenegro, the only republics not seceding from Yugoslavia, created a new, smaller rump Yugoslavia. Finally, in July 1992, the substantial Croat minority in Bosnia and Herzegovina proclaimed the Croatian Community of Herceg-Bosnia.

Although the relatively homogeneous Slovenia skirmished with Yugoslavia over its independence, the real wars came in Croatia and Bosnia. Not coincidentally, the problem stemmed from significant minorities of Serbs left in the Krajina region of Croatia and Croatians and Serbs left in Bosnia and Herzegovina. The secession of Slovenia and Croatia also raised fears of Serb domination in the rump Yugoslavia over the remaining Albanians, Macedonians, and Bosnian Muslims, sparking the subsequent secessionist movements.[201] Even Slobodan Milosevic, then president of the Serbs, at first refused to recognize the supremacy of Yugoslavia's eight-member presidency.[202] (He later became president of the new rump Yugoslavia.)

In Yugoslavia, a mosaic of ethnicities existed in every region except Slovenia, where not coincidentally the least violence upon declaration of independence occurred in the otherwise bloody Yugoslav wars of secession. Because of its homogeneous population of Slovenes, Slovenia's secessionist demands didn't pose much of a threat to the rest of Yugoslavia.[203] In contrast, the political boundaries of the rest of the new independent states left substantial minorities on opposing sides of division lines, creating multiple security dilemmas. At the other extreme from Slovenia, Bosnia and Herzegovina had such large minority groups that no majority group existed—32 percent of the Bosnian population was Serb, 18 percent was Croat, and 39 percent was Bosnian Muslim. Consequently, of any successor country, Bosnia had the most violence upon independence from Yugoslavia. Croatia, with a 12 percent Serb population, also experienced some violence upon independence. According to Laslo Sekelj, "For Serbia . . . the most important consequence of the break-up of the former Yugoslavia was that a significant part (25%) of the Serbian nation remained in Croatia and in Bosnia-Herzegovina—against their own free will—without the state links with Serbia they had since 1918."[204]

As a result of the incomplete partitions in most of the new states of the former Yugoslavia, the Yugoslav wars of secession killed more than a hundred thousand people—some in brutal atrocities not seen since

Hitler's Germany—and created two million refugees. In contrast, the fact that Czechs populated only 1 percent of Slovak lands and Slovaks lived on only 3 percent of the Czech lands facilitated a peaceful breakup of Czechoslovakia.

In another illustration of the difference in results between incomplete and virtually complete partitions, the rump Yugoslavia (Serbia and Montenegro) was composed of 63 percent Serbs, 13.5 percent Albanians, and 5.5 percent Montenegrins.[205] Violence and war ensued as the substantial minority Albanian population, an overwhelming majority in the province of Kosovo, effectively broke away from Yugoslavia. In contrast, the small minority of Montenegrins, ethnically and culturally similar to the Serbs, eventually seceded, but it was peaceful.

Another case showing the difficulty of an incomplete partition and the ease of a virtually complete division—all in one country—is the partition of Ireland in 1921. A substantial Catholic minority—34 percent—was trapped in the six counties of Northern Ireland (an incomplete partition), thus threatening the fairly commingled Protestant majority there and leading to decades of violence. Protestants feared Catholic rule or the union of Northern Ireland with predominantly Catholic Ireland. In contrast, in the rest of Ireland, a small, thinly dispersed minority of Protestants—less than 10 percent—has lived in peace for decades with the overwhelming Catholic majority (thus constituting a virtually complete partition). The minority was no military or political threat to the majority. Thus the partition of Ireland per se was not the cause of the violence in the North. If the British had drawn the partition line between Ireland and Northern Ireland so that fewer Catholics were stranded north of the border, far less violence would probably have ensued over the decades.[206]

Similarly, on the Indian subcontinent, violence during the partition centered in the northwest in Punjab province, where the significant, evenly spread, wealthy, and well-armed Sikh minority lived and had their important religious sites. The Sikhs did not want to be ruled by Muslims in what was to become Pakistan. As in Iraq, Punjab had well-armed militias and a fear of domination by the "other." The Sikhs wanted either to have an independent state or be within India; the Muslims rejected both proposals, which would have required significant population movements. The incomplete partition agreement sending West Punjab to Pakistan and East Punjab to India would have left almost two million Sikhs stranded in Pakistan. The Sikhs executed a preplanned evacuation from West Punjab to the east and ethnically cleansed Muslim populations forcibly from East Punjab. The conflict in Punjab caused retaliatory rounds of ethnic cleansing in surrounding provinces and in Pakistan.

Although the partition met the legitimate demand from a large group of Muslims for self-determination and separation from Hindu-dominated India, a poorly drawn partition line, which denied that same self-determination to the Sikhs, resulted in one of the largest campaigns of ethnic cleansing in world history. Hundreds of thousands of people died and ten to twelve million people became refugees. Yet widespread and lethal violence occurred before the partition,[207] and it could have been even worse if India and Pakistan had not been divided. According to Yasmin Khan, the author of *The Great Partition,* "It is not implausible that South Asia could have spiraled into an even more devastating civil war."[208] The Sikhs later campaigned for a further partition of Punjab in order to break off a province within India containing a Sikh majority. The Indian government wisely made that happen in 1966.

Also in the west, Jammu-Kashmir could have been partitioned more easily than Punjab or even Bengal in the east, because most of the Hindus were concentrated in Jammu, the southernmost part near India; however, the British did not divide the area. In 1948, a war over the area resulted between the new countries of India and Pakistan, which led to the incorporation of a large Jammu-Kashmiri population that was two-thirds Muslim into Hindu India—an incomplete partition that was a recipe for trouble. A more stable and complete partition would have given most of Jammu-Kashmir to Pakistan, but India's thirst for territory was too great.

Since the war, two additional Indo-Pakistani conflicts and even nuclear threats have arisen over Jammu-Kashmir. Even today, about sixty years after the first war, violence in the region is still endemic. Muslim separatist groups, with assistance from Pakistan, want either to gain independence or join Muslim Pakistan.

During the partition of the subcontinent in 1947, in the princely Indian states of Alwar and Bharatpur, which had Hindu majorities, the Muslim group there, the Meos, which constituted large minorities, were either killed or ethnically cleansed from these areas. About thirty thousand Muslims were killed, and one hundred thousand fled the states.[209]

In contrast, the virtually complete division of West Bengal into India and East Bengal into East Pakistan (now Bangladesh) helped reduce violence in the eastern part of the subcontinent. The partition did not strand large minorities of Hindus or Muslims on the wrong side of the dividing line. Intercommunal violence stopped after the partition and successful movement of 3.5 million people with little carnage.

Although occasional violence still occurs among Hindus and Muslims in non–Jammu-Kashmiri India, population transfers at the time of partition have probably prevented much greater violence since the late 1940s in Pakistan and most of India. In non–Jammu-Kashmiri India, the Muslim population is diffused enough in most of the country so as not to be a major threat to the Hindus. In Pakistan, very few Hindus remained after the partition and have not presented a security dilemma to the overwhelming majority of Muslims there.[210] Both of these are virtually complete partitions, and both have been largely successful. In contrast, it is no coincidence that Jammu-Kashmir, which was not partitioned and has a concentrated and substantial minority Muslim population in a Hindu country, is where the continuing large-scale violence occurs.

The difficulty for a large ethnic group of living peacefully in a country run by another such group also can be seen in the case of Malaysia. In 1957, Malaya gained independence from the British Empire. Non-Malays, mostly ethnic Chinese, could be given Malay citizenship without upsetting Malay political dominance, thus ensuring a peaceful partition from the empire. In contrast, when the overwhelmingly Chinese Singapore joined with Malaya to form Malaysia in 1963, its addition created a situation in which non-Malays outnumbered Malays (who were then only 40 percent of the combined population)—thus threatening Malay political supremacy. It is not surprising then that race riots ensued in 1964 and the Malays expelled Singapore from Malaysia in 1965 to avoid further ethnic turbulence. The preventive partition worked and mass violence was avoided.[211]

Even in cases where significant violence occurred during or after a partition—that is, in Ireland, the Indian subcontinent, the nations of the former Yugoslavia, and Palestine (see below)—the division probably reduced the overall strife from what it might have been without the separation of warring factions. In three out of the four cases, significant violence occurred before the partition. For example, before the partition of Ireland in 1921, a major revolt by Irish Catholics had been put down in 1916, and tensions still smoldered. Similarly, before the partition of South Asia in 1947, a civil war between Hindus, Sikhs, and Muslims had already erupted in 1946.[212] Before the partition of Palestine in 1947,[213] violence between Jews and Arabs had been going on since the 1920s. Moreover, much of the violence that resulted subsequent to each of these divisions was because the partition was incomplete—that is, the dividing line between hostile populations left a significant concentrated minority in a majority area—not because of the separation itself.

A partition of Iraq has one major advantage over the violent partition of the Indian subcontinent. Britain artificially forced the jumble of communities and nationalities contained in the British Raj into the two states of Muslim Pakistan and Hindu India.[214] In contrast, in Iraq, except for the major cities that are more mixed, the three ethno-sectarian groups—the Kurds, Sunnis, and Shi'a—predominate in specific parts of the country. The Kurds live in the north, the Sunnis in central Iraq, and the Shi'a in the southern part of the country. (Because of intra-group tensions, however, each of these regions might need to be subdivided into autonomous areas.) As noted earlier, even the cities have become less mixed as ethnic cleansing and other violence has created more homogeneous areas. Although some people would still have to move, the more distinct ethno-sectarian areas in Iraq—as compared with populations in the Indian subcontinent—should make the population transfers smaller, easier, and less violent.

In the north, the Kurds' autonomous region, which they have governed separately from Iraq since the end of the first Gulf War in 1991, doesn't encompass all of the Kurdish areas. The borders between Kurdistan and any Sunni autonomous region could be gerrymandered to allow the Kurds to include such Kurdish areas in their autonomous region in exchange for giving the Sunnis some of their oil-rich areas, which lie along the boundary between Kurdish and Sunni lands. Such border gerrymandering would make the oil-poor Sunnis more receptive to the idea of partitioning Iraq.

5. Boundaries Should Also Consider Resources and Cultural and Religious Sites

Dividing resources can often be a major issue when executing a partition. For example, during the dividing of Punjab province when India and Pakistan separated, there existed an interlocking web of canals—needed for the region's prosperity—which the partition threatened with dismemberment.[215] In Yugoslavia, Slovenia, and Croatia, the wealthier parts of the country, became tired of subsidizing the other regions and were the first to secede.[216] Similarly, the wealthier Czechs got tired of subsidizing the poorer Slovaks and essentially kicked them out of Czechoslovakia. Belgium may eventually break up for the same reason: the wealthier Dutch-speaking Flemish feel that they are subsidizing the poorer French-speaking Walloons.

In Iraq, although support for decentralization is growing among Sunnis, they still are more reluctant to support it than the other groups because their territory has fewer known oil reserves (that is, they are relatively resource-poor) than the Kurds in the north and the Shi'a in the south. The key source of revenue for Iraq is oil. This commodity accounts for 90 percent or more of the country's exports.[217] Iraq has the second-largest known oil reserves in the world. Its oil patches are located west of Kirkuk—a city in the north outside the current Kurdish enclave, but which the Kurds desire as their future capital—and in the Shi'i areas of the south. Any plan to decentralize Iraq in the form of a confederation or partition into independent states might go up in the flames of a civil war if an agreement is not reached on the sharing of oil revenues among factions.[218] The squabble over the multi-ethnic city of Kirkuk, coveted by several groups, might also prove explosive.[219]

Of course, oil resources are often a curse for countries because they offer a crutch from the difficult economic reforms that are needed for long-term prosperity; conversely, nations can prosper without a great endowment of natural resources—for example, Japan. Yet these facts will probably not dissuade the Sunnis from trying to get some of Iraq's oil. Furthermore, one independent oil research firm claims that it has discovered massive oil reserves in Sunni lands in Al-Anbar province.[220] Nevertheless, at this writing, the assumption has to be that the Sunnis don't have much oil on their territory and this current reality will affect their views on decentralization.

The Shi'a have about 60 percent of Iraq's population and about 60 percent of the known oil reserves. The Kurds, who have about 20 percent of the country's population, as well as the other 40 percent of the oil reserves, want to expand their autonomous region to bring more of the Kurdish population under its jurisdiction. The Sunnis would be much more likely to accept decentralization if they were given half of the Kurds' oil reserves so that they would have 20 percent of Iraq's oil reserves to match their 20 percent of the population. Thus, only the northern border between Kurdistan and any Sunni autonomous region would have to be altered, not the southern border between the Sunni and Shi'i autonomous regions. Yet where exactly the border should run in the north may be fiercely contested in partition negotiations, because of the oil resources under the ground and the Kurdish populations on top of it. But solving this dispute peacefully—hopefully with the aforementioned trade—will be critical to the success of the negotiations.

Right now, the Shi'a and Kurds, in the driver's seat of the Iraqi central government, have no incentive to make concessions to the Sunni population to achieve ambitious decentralization. But if the United States threatened to rapidly withdraw its troops—pulling the last crutch out from the nonviable, incompetent, corrupt, and sectarian Iraqi central government—these two ruling groups, to avoid a full-blown civil war, would have more of an incentive to negotiate a decentralization agreement with the Sunnis.

Some advocates of partition want to punish the Sunnis for their resistance to the U.S. occupation and to reward the Kurds and Shi'a for being more cooperative.[221] But that is a recipe for disaster. If the Sunnis feel more secure and feel fairly treated, they will be less likely to resist a settlement. Cutting the Sunnis out of Iraq's oil revenues might lead to a bloody civil war, the worst possible outcome. In departing Iraq, the United States should quietly mediate an agreement on oil sharing that is satisfactory to all three groups and an arrangement on the city of Kirkuk that is acceptable to the Kurds, Sunni Arabs, and other minorities. Alternatively, agreement among all Iraqi groups on a respected, independent mediator might be regarded as a less-biased option. The agreement that ended the civil war in southern Sudan contains such a revenue-sharing arrangement for oil and other resources.[222] Thus there is hope that a peaceful agreement can also be negotiated in Iraq.

As for land containing cultural, religious, and other "intangible" sites, it is often contested more fiercely than territory of strategic or economic significance. Compromising over or substituting for such emotionally laden ground is often difficult for groups to do.[223] For example, during the partitioning of the Indian subcontinent, the ill-drawn boundary lines left the holiest Sikh pilgrimage sites within Muslim-dominated Pakistan, which contributed to violence by the well-armed Sikhs.[224]

Cultural and religious sites have been a major sticking point in the partition of the Albanian-dominated province of Kosovo from Serbia, which occurred after the NATO air war against Serbia in 1999. Although there has been some sporadic violence between the 94 percent Muslim Albanian population and the 6 percent Christian Serbian population of Kosovo, this small minority of Serbs is not a threat to the security of the majority Albanian population. Even greater than Serbia's fear that the Albanian majority will persecute the Serb minority in Kosovo is its concern that the cradle of Serb civilization is in the breakaway province. The Serbs consider Kosovo sacred because it contains religious and historical Serb sites.

Unfortunately, the United Nations plan for Kosovar independence only "protects" the Serb shrines, while leaving them in an Albanian-dominated Kosovo.[225] This outcome is unacceptable to the Serbs and could lead to a later resumption of violence. The international community should heed Russia's preference and also partition Kosovo, with the shrines and heavily Serb-populated areas being given back to Serbia. For the long term, the Albanians would receive a slightly smaller, but much more secure, Kosovo.

Similarly, the status of Jerusalem, sacred to both the Jewish and Islamic faiths, continues to be one of the major stumbling blocks to rectifying the botched partition of Palestine in 1947. Another is the desire of militant Jews to enlarge, through settlements on occupied Arab land, what in their minds is the biblically sacred land of Israel, and the violent Arab opposition to this expansion.

The problem in any Iraqi partition of adjusting the borders for cultural sites is much less severe than in Pakistan, Kosovo, or Palestine. Iraq is the cradle of Shi'i Islam, but the religious centers are already in Shi'i-controlled areas in the south. Thus the border between any Sunni and Shi'i autonomous regions would not have to be adjusted for this reason. However, competing Shi'i groups might want the shrines in their own areas, which could spark intra-Shi'i violence. Therefore a negotiation among the groups might be needed to establish governance over the shrines and pilgrimage rights to them.

6. Regions Should Be Defensible
but Don't Necessarily Have to Be Contiguous

Jews and Arabs had been fighting over Palestine since the 1920s. By the time the British left Palestine in 1948, the Jews had settled in three noncontiguous areas: in Jerusalem, by the Sea of Galilee, and on a coastal strip along the Mediterranean Sea from Haifa to Tel Aviv. All-Arab areas surrounded the three Jewish areas, and the Jews were worried about defending the road from the coastal areas to the Jewish sector of Jerusalem, which was under siege.[226] The United Nations partition plan did not help matters by giving both the Jews and the Arabs three non-defensible, noncontiguous pieces of land. The ensuing war in 1948 made the three Jewish areas contiguous by capturing the spaces between them and, through additional ethnic cleansing, created a new state with an 85 percent Jewish majority.

Re-intermingling the two populations has led to more recent bloodshed (since 1967). A heavily armed Jewish minority has been established in settlements in the midst of the majority Arab populations in the West Bank and Gaza (the latter outposts have been withdrawn).[227] Such noncontiguous Jewish settlements take yet more Palestinian land and are defended by a new Israeli wall and Israeli army restrictions on Arab movements between their towns. Such barriers and restrictions cause even more friction between the Jewish minority and the Arab majority. The wall encloses about 15 percent of the occupied West Bank—that is, it encompasses a population of several hundred thousand Palestinians and makes them de facto part of Israel. In the short term, the wall has reduced anti-Israeli terrorism, but in the long term the substantial and stranded Palestinian minority will likely create more Israeli-Palestinian hostility, which could end in escalating violence.[228] If instead the wall had been created after a comprehensive Israeli-Palestinian settlement and had been erected along a mutually agreed boundary between Israel and a new independent Palestinian state, it might have been regarded as a constructive development. Now the unilaterally built wall, and the large Palestinian population trapped on the wrong side, could be flashpoints for future violence.

Ideally, war or ethnic cleansing can be avoided by creating defensible contiguous areas by agreement. Yet that may not always be possible, especially if population patterns don't allow it. Certainly it is better from a security standpoint to have contiguous areas, but small enclaves can be economically viable—for example, Luxembourg, Lichtenstein, Singapore, and Hong Kong are all small areas that are economically vibrant because they are connected to the globalized economy through trade and investment flows.

To the extent that Iraq's autonomous regions could be made up of contiguous lands, that would be the preferable outcome. But in Iraq, oil fields or certain other pieces of land with homogeneous populations might have to be left unattached to majority areas of that same population group. The fact that small minorities do not usually cause security threats to majorities and likely could be left safely in their areas, however, may make it possible to keep the number of specially designated homogeneous noncontiguous areas to a minimum. Again, the historical record shows that partitions don't have to be perfect to provide peace and prosperity for the populations involved.

If Iraq is divided into more than three autonomous regions—as is likely because the reality on the ground is already one of numerous autonomous city-states—homogeneous noncontiguous areas could stand alone instead of being affiliated with larger areas of like populations. This would be especially true if Iraq becomes an economic confederation with a unified market.

7. Population Movements May Be Necessary, but They Must Be Voluntary

Partition without separating most of a population, that is, incomplete partitions, can result in violence—as in the examples of Ireland, Palestine, the Indian subcontinent, and when Croatia and Bosnia seceded from Yugoslavia. Yet because the international community has many multi-ethnic states that don't want the principle of state sovereignty undermined, it has long been self-servingly reluctant to endorse autonomy, partition, and the movement of substantial populations, even when violent conflict among ethno-sectarian groups occurs. For example, the United Nations High Commissioner for Refugees (UNHCR) wants to bring "safety to people, not people to safety."[229] Pursuing this politically correct goal oftentimes gets the people slaughtered that the international community is trying to help.

During the partition of the Indian subcontinent, neither the Pakistanis nor the Indians wanted to promote population movements or even give them legitimacy. In fact, the authorities of the two new governments initially tried to stop population movements in order to maintain large minorities of their ethno-sectarian kinsmen on the other state's soil in a sort of mutual hostage-holding against discrimination and persecution of minorities. The British also did their part to impede population migration. Until the last minute, the British were deliberately vague about where the partition boundary lines would run and then did not make clear whether people should move to the country in which their coreligionists were in the majority. Fear of being left on the wrong side of the line made people vote with their feet and rendered governmental planning and policy null and void. Large numbers of refugees began to move even before partition, and the quantities increased after it was announced. Governmental discouragement of migration and uncertainty surrounding the details of the partition merely escalated the violence and ethnic cleansing for which leaders were ill prepared. [230]

In the international community, there is reluctance by many to legitimize the nearly homogeneous ethno-sectarian enclaves created by ethnic cleansing and then reinforce this division with additional voluntary population movements. In fact, many in the international community often endanger the people they purport to help by advocating the reintegration of the formerly multi-ethnic state—encouraging or forcing the return of refugees after a cease-fire takes hold.[231] For example, after the war in Bosnia, the international community made a great effort to encourage ethno-sectarian minority refugees to return to their homes in areas now dominated by majorities of other ethno-sectarian groups; nearly a half million out of a total Bosnian population of 3.5 million did so.[232] Yet the intermingling of ethno-sectarian populations produced by such reintegration may yet prove to be a mistake if it eventually causes a resumption of the ethnic violence in that country.

Some evidence, however, exists that the reverse—movements of large minority populations into enclaves already dominated by their own ethno-sectarian group—has saved lives. After the post–World War I Bulgarian, Greek, and Turkish population transfers and the Eastern European expulsion of Germans after World War II, peace ensued in both of these war-torn areas.[233]

Partition can reduce the need for most population migration. Even with the best-drawn borders during a partition, however, some population movements may be necessary. Forced population migrations are a violation of human rights, but voluntary ones are not. People in minority groups on the wrong side of a partition line may feel insecure and thus voluntarily move across the line to areas where their group is in the majority. Some such population movements may have to happen in Iraqi cities and other intermingled areas. To encourage groups of people to move, the Iraqi government or some other government could provide monetary incentives to them.

Some opponents of partition, and the population movements associated with it, have used the inflammatory label of "apartheid" to condemn it. But apartheid in South Africa was imposed with guns on the majority by a powerful minority. Any Iraqi partition, and accompanying population movements, must be voluntary and part of a genuine policy of allowing Iraqis true self-determination.

8. Adequate Security Must Be Provided for the Population Movements

During the partition of the Indian subcontinent, many refugees were killed because they were routed through the war zone in Punjab. For example, the Sikhs killed many Muslims as they crossed through Sikh territory by train. The authorities should have routed the trains around the war zone or provided adequate security forces to guard the refugees, but they failed to do so. As noted earlier, they were unprepared for large population migrations and actually initially discouraged them, but the people voted with their feet because they feared discrimination, harassment, and even death as stranded minorities on the other side of the new international dividing lines. Because the partition was top down, ethno-sectarian militias, instead of protecting refugees, were creating and ethnically cleansing them.[234]

In Iraq, a non–U.S. international peacekeeping force or militia members from the group being moved should provide security for the migrants. An international force—if it can be arranged—might be better since the guarding militia might get into a tussle with another group's militia while transiting the latter's territory. If an internationally recognized settlement among all ethno-sectarian groups for Iraqi decentralization could be reached and the violence attenuated, it would be much easier to assemble an international force for the job of refugee protection. Because of all the bad blood in Iraq generated by the U.S. occupation, an international force would be better off without U.S. participation. The United States, however, could provide behind-the-scenes intelligence and logistical support for the force.

9. A Decentralized Iraq Does Not Need to Have Only Three Autonomous Regions

Just because three main ethno-sectarian groups exist in Iraq, there don't have to be only three autonomous areas. In some cases, borders might need to be drawn on tribal boundaries; cities that still pride themselves on their cosmopolitan outlook could remain as heterogeneous autonomous regions. The Kurdish north or the Shi'i south could split into more than one region. In fact, as noted earlier, Iraq is already a conglomeration of autonomous city-states, with various local militias providing security and other services. The important thing is that a national conclave should be held in which all Iraqi groups can negotiate the specifics of decentralization and its implementation.

10. If Any Central Government Remains, It Must Be Weak

Iraq's history is of one ethno-sectarian group (the Sunnis) controlling a strong central government and using it to dominate and repress the other groups. Much of the sectarian violence now occurring in Iraq is a result of fears that this could happen again. As Anna Morawiec Mansfield notes in the *Columbia Law Review*, "Constitutions in ethnically divided countries must become instruments to limit governmental power."[235]

Although Iraq's post-invasion constitution is fairly decentralized, it is still not decentralized enough. The Shi'a and Kurds now control the central government, and the Sunnis are afraid of payback for their days in control. This fear has ample justification, given that Shi'i militia death squads associated with the Iraqi security forces have executed large numbers of Sunnis. The Shi'a, although in the majority, fear that the Sunnis will try to regain power and oppress them again. In contrast, the Kurds, in their largely peaceful autonomous northern bastion, have less fear of the other groups—illustrating the security advantages of decentralization and separation. There has been some tension and violence in Mosul and Kirkuk, cities with mixed populations of Sunni Arabs and Kurds, that might benefit from an adjustment of the border between Kurdistan and Sunni territories and voluntary population movements.

Taking a lesson from the Kurds, if the Sunnis and Shi'a, through an agreement to partition Iraq, received autonomous regions and the central government was rendered weak or nonexistent, the sectarian violence would likely plummet permanently. Fears of repression by a strong central government controlled by a rival group would lessen. In other words, good fences make good neighbors.

If decentralization is accepted as a policy, then the question might arise: What should be the endpoint of a partition—a loose, decentralized confederation of autonomous regions or outright division into three or more new states?

A loose Iraqi confederation might very well be a waypoint to eventual independent statehood for the autonomous regions. Power to both the Czechoslovak[236] and Yugoslav federations was greatly decentralized, but eventually they broke up anyway.[237] Yet such a weak Iraqi central government wouldn't threaten any of the ethno-sectarian groups with oppression, so they might have less of an incentive to seek independence.

Turkey has attacked and threatened to invade Iraqi Kurdistan to eliminate sanctuaries for Turkish Kurds attacking targets in Turkey. A confederation of autonomous regions in Iraq might be more reassuring to Turkey than an independent Kurdish state, which could act as a beacon for Kurdish secession from Turkey. The Turks must know that although they might not be enthusiastic about a decentralized Iraqi confederation, there are worse outcomes than those of a "soft" partition into confederation. If a full-blown Iraqi civil war were to erupt, the Kurds would likely use that conflict as an excuse to declare an independent Kurdish state,[238] a worse outcome for Turkey. Turkey is also restrained by its bountiful investment in Iraqi Kurdistan, its alliance with the United States in NATO, and its bid to get into the European Union, which would be torpedoed—by Europeans already eager to nix it—in the wake of any Turkish invasion of Iraq.

Furthermore, a confederation, rather than the independence of smaller new states, might at least marginally reduce Iranian influence in the Shi'i south. Either a confederation or new independent states would limit Iranian influence to southern Iraq; now Iran has influence over an Iraqi central government that, at least theoretically, governs all of Iraq. At the margins, Iran might have more influence over a new independent state in the south controlled by the Shi'a than over a Shi'i autonomous region that still had some ties (mainly economic) to other areas in Iraq.

Although Bosnia should not be taken as a model for nation building, what stability exists there now is due to decentralization in the form of a confederation between a Muslim-Croat federation and the Serb Republic of Srpska. The reason for the stability is that these sub-entities have nearly homogeneous ethnic components.[239] The Republic of Srpska is extremely autonomous, and the Muslim-Croat federation has ten cantons, eight of which have a prominent Muslim or Croat majority. Two out of three ethnic groups in Bosnia—the Croats and Serbs—rejected an integrated unitary state, while only a slim majority of the Bosnian Muslims preferred this outcome.[240] In Bosnia, the reality has confirmed a growing body of commonsense scholarship, which argues that separating warring groups reduces violence and intermingling them escalates conflict.[241]

The central government of the Bosnian confederation is weak, its component governments are strong and enjoy great autonomy, and each ethnic community effectively has a veto over the remaining functions of that central entity (that is, the central government is consociational). There is a three-person presidency, with a member from each group, and each chamber of the bicameral Bosnian legislature has equal representation from each group.[242] The majority Bosniaks want a stronger central government, but the Serbs fear this outcome[243] for much the same reason that the Sunnis fear it in Iraq: majority paybacks for prior dominance and oppression. Further centralization, however, would probably result in more violence among the Bosnian groups.

In any event, although decentralized, the consociational Bosnian government arising out of the Dayton accords is probably still too strong. Westerners, who considered an outright partition into three new states[244] (similar to the division of Yugoslavia[245] and the later partition of Kosovo from Serbia), set up the government. But in the end, the Western powers remained enamored with the politically correct goal of retaining the trappings of a multi-ethnic society. In fact, in contrast to the international community's more realistic goals in the nations of the former Yugoslavia and Kosovo, where division has been accepted in both cases, the world would like to see a slow genuine reintegration of Bosnia into a multi-ethnic state.[246] In the interest of "nation building," the international community has violated the Dayton Agreement—with its wise emphasis on the critical function of law enforcement remaining at the local level (a confederation arrangement)—by creating multi-ethnic police forces controlled from the center. This centralization (federalization) of policing requires officers of one ethno-sectarian group to police the area of another—likely exacerbating existing ethno-sectarian tensions over the long term, and perhaps even leading to renewed civil war.[247] The road to hell is often paved with good intentions.

The reality in Bosnia is that outside powers ordered the partition and large minority populations are a threat to the plurality of Muslims and to each other. Furthermore, despite their relatively homogeneous enclaves, these large minorities—the Bosnian Croats and Serbs—have special relationships (for example, dual citizenship enshrined in the Dayton Agreement) with and would actually like to be part of neighboring Croatia and Serbia, respectively. Bosnian Croat dissatisfaction with the Bosnian Muslim-Croat federation led to a rebellion in 2001. Consociationalism may work in countries with some national identity and no recent strife—for example, Switzerland—but it is less viable in societies with great ethno-sectarian cleavages, such as Bosnia.[248] Because control over the still too-strong Bosnian central government is important to the various groups, a return to violence remains a possibility in Bosnia.

If, as Sumantra Bose concludes, "In post-Yugoslavia and post-war Bosnia, where 'nation-building' integration is a fantasy, at once hopelessly naïve and mindlessly arrogant,"[249] the same is true for Iraq. To reduce such violence in an Iraqi society equally cleaved by ethno-sectarian animosities, a framework of consociationalism should be avoided or restricted to the minimal number of functions the central government is allowed to retain in any confederation. Thus in Iraq, if a confederation is chosen—mainly as a veneer so that Turkey doesn't feel compelled to invade Iraqi Kurdistan—the central government should be made as weak as possible.

The Iraqi Constitution already provides for significant decentralization. Article III states that Iraq's regions hold any powers that the Constitution does not give exclusively to the central government. The document also states that in any conflict arising between the laws of the central government and regional governments, regional legislation will prevail (unlike the Supremacy Clause of the U.S. Constitution, which says that conflicts between federal and state law will be resolved in favor of the federal statute). In fact, Article 13 of the Iraqi Constitution says that in areas outside the exclusive powers of the Iraqi central government, the regions can amend central laws that conflict with regional law.[250]

Certainly control over security and law enforcement (that is, militias), the judiciary, tax collection, the currency, the economy, and natural resources should all be exercised at the local level. Otherwise the ethno-sectarian groups will probably engage in sectarian violence for control of the central government. Any guns, and forces possessing them, under the control of the central government will cause deep fears at the regional level. Article 129 of the Iraqi Constitution already allows regional security forces;[251] thus the U.S. fantasy of creating truly "national" security forces should be abandoned and the Iraqi army and police disbanded—this time permanently. In Iraqi Kurdistan, it has been demonstrated that local militias of the same ethno-sectarian group as the population can keep the peace nicely. Similarly, in the aftermath of the U.S. invasion, Shi'i militias maintained security in Shi'i areas. Furthermore, much of the recent reduction in violence in the rest of Iraq, claimed to be due to the U.S. surge in troop numbers, has more to do with U.S. forces working with, and not against, local militias—for example, with local Sunni forces in Anbar and Amiriya and with local Shi'i militias in some parts of Baghdad.[252]

Similarly, judicial processes and decisions will not be perceived as fair unless the judicial systems are under local control. As for oil, the Sunnis will probably lack trust in the Kurds and Shi'a to honor, in the long term, an arrangement for sharing oil revenues. Thus, as noted earlier, the boundary between Kurdistan and any Sunni autonomous region would need to be gerrymandered to give the Kurdish autonomous region control over more Kurdish-populated lands in exchange for giving Sunnis some Kurdish oil fields.

In short, a central government might be limited to maintaining an internal free trade area within Iraq, negotiating trade agreements with other nations, and providing an Iraqi diplomatic presence overseas. For example, after the breakup of Czechoslovakia, interstate agreements between Slovakia and the Czech Republic included the creation of a customs union and monetary arrangements that would facilitate the conversion of currency.[253] Even in terms of diplomatic services, Iraq is already unique in the world, because Article 116 of its Constitution provides for regional representation at its embassies abroad.[254]

Finally, despite these suggestions, having the United States or the international community dictate the partition—as was done in Bosnia—to ensure that every item in this book's recommendations is checked off would be a disaster. The United States and the international community should regard suggestion number two—An Outside Power Cannot Impose a Sustainable Partition—as being the most important and the prime directive.

11. Peacefully Negotiated Partitions Reduce International Conflict

Critics allege that partitions lead to more interstate war. Such conflict could conceivably come in two forms. First, an incomplete partition could occur, leading to large minorities or religious or cultural sites stranded across the dividing line—thus potentially igniting war between the successor states containing the majority enclaves of the ethno-sectarian groups. This problem often occurs when the international community applies pressure to use the old internal administrative boundaries within the original state as the new international borders of successor states.[255]

Quantitative statistical research by Jaroslav Tir, a political scientist, shows that peaceful partitions are much more successful at reducing post-partition violence than violent partitions. Tir has two categories— violently partitioned countries and preventive, peaceful partitions. Partitions that result from ethnic conflict result in a decrease in domestic violence within the new states and avoid militarized international disputes with each other 37.5 percent of the time and avoid full-blown international wars 62.5 percent of the time. In peaceful preventive partitions, 54.5 percent of resulting states escape internal conflict, and they avoid militarized international disputes with each other 93.5 percent of the time and international wars 100 percent of the time.[256]

An example of a preventive partition that avoided imminent violence between ethno-sectarian groups was Malaysia's break with Singapore in 1965. The resulting international tension between the two separated states was better than a domestic bloodbath under a combined country, which was portended by racial riots in 1964.[257] In the case of Czechoslovakia, the country was peacefully partitioned, and the successor states of the Czech Republic and Slovakia later agreed to change their border without violence.[258]

The key ambiguity is whether Iraq's level of sectarian violence has risen to the point where it would fit into the category of a violent partition rather than a peaceful one. At the time of this writing, Iraq has experienced significant sectarian violence, but not a full-blown civil war. Recently, the violence in Iraq has decreased. In a later article, however, Tir clarifies what he sees as the difference between violent and peaceful partitions. In a violent partition, the victor imposes the boundary line on the vanquished, whereas in a peaceful partition all sides negotiate and concur on the border.[259] As already noted in lesson number two, if all parties agree on the partition in advance, there is a dramatic increase in the likelihood of its success.

In Iraq today, any partition still would have to be a preventive one, reached by a compromise among the ethno-sectarian groups, which would attempt to reduce or end future sectarian strife. Thus despite the ongoing (but reduced) violence, an Iraqi partition would not be imposed and thus would fit into the category of a peaceful division in Tir's taxonomy. International conflicts would likely be dramatically reduced by any negotiated breakup of Iraq.

Partition of Iraq into a loose confederation aims to avoid a bloody civil war, which could draw in neighboring countries to support their corresponding ethno-sectarian groups—for example, Syria, Jordan,

Egypt, and Saudi Arabia backing the Sunnis; Iran supporting the Shi'a; and Israel assisting the Kurds. Thus if partition were successful in avoiding an all-out internecine conflict, it would also lower the probability of a regional war.

In any case, partition combined with a complete U.S. withdrawal seems worth a try, especially if Herculean efforts are made to follow the lessons of history spelled out in this paper—for example, getting all parties to agree to the division in advance and drawing boundary lines between the ethno-sectarian regions in order to equitably share oil resources and to avoid large minority populations being stranded on the wrong side of the dividing lines. The alternative is almost assuredly U.S. entrapment in a quagmire of escalating long-term sectarian violence under the current dysfunctional Iraqi system of central governance. As in Vietnam, the United States could enhance its international standing by withdrawing. Ending U.S. occupation of one Muslim land while stabilizing the country—which partition has the best chance of achieving—would also undoubtedly reduce Islamist attacks on U.S. targets worldwide, which are primarily revenge for non-Muslim meddling in Muslim lands.

The second way a partition could allegedly increase international conflict is as a precedent and inspiration for other ethno-sectarian groups to secede from their parent states. The international community, made of many states containing multiple ethno-sectarian groups, is understandably very uneasy about secession in other places in the world. For example, in 1971, when India, a leader in the nonaligned movement, invaded East Pakistan to liberate it from the dominance of West Pakistan and ensure its demanded self-determination—traditionally a primary concern of nonaligned nations when exercised vis-à-vis Western colonial powers—very few of the more than sixty nonaligned countries supported India diplomatically.[260]

More recent successful secession attempts have caused similar international unease. The successful secession of Kosovo from Serbia has caused some fears of ethno-sectarian groups in other countries following this lead and provoking wars of independence against their governments. For example, states with restive ethno-sectarian minorities—such as Spain, Cyprus, and Romania—were not supportive of Kosovo's bid for independence, and such minorities have used Kosovo's success to attempt to gain legitimacy for their own similar bids—such as Hungarians in Romania and South Ossetians in the Republic of Georgia. Furthermore, the secession of Eritrea from Ethiopia, the former Soviet republics from the USSR, the former Yugoslav republics from that nation, and the peaceful breakup of Czechoslovakia have also heightened anxieties in the international arena.

Such fears may, however, be overblown. Milica Z. Bookman found that over the past two centuries, successful secessionist efforts have been fairly rare.[261] Similarly, A. Heraclides studied seventy wars of secession but found that only five were successful.[262] Such a track record of ineffectiveness may dissuade some ethno-sectarian groups from employing this strategy, instead encouraging peaceful ways of redressing their grievances with central authorities.

In the wake of an Iraqi partition, even if the chances of international conflict increase for either of these two reasons—as unlikely as that outcome is—the drawbacks have to be balanced against the U.S. need to extricate itself from a costly predicament (in terms of casualties and money) that endangers the U.S. homeland by inflaming radical Islamist terrorism. Furthermore, ethnic civil wars are usually bloodier than interstate conflicts because the domestic groups believe that the winner(s) of the civil war will use the central government to oppress the losing group(s). In contrast, in most interstate wars, the outcome of the conflict results in merely a shift in boundaries of existing states.

12. Powerful Neighbors Must Be Brought into the Partition Process

In the Bosnian partition, the leaders of neighboring Serbia (Slobodan Milosevic) and Croatia (Franjo Tudjman)—sponsors of the Bosnian

Serbs and Bosnian Croats, respectively, in the civil war—were wisely brought into the negotiation of the Dayton Agreement.[263] In the case of Iraq, surrounding countries with stakes in an Iraqi partition will have to be included in the partition negotiations. Jordan, Saudi Arabia, Turkey, Syria, and Iran will all need to participate in the conclave. This will greatly reduce the prospect of a partition causing an international conflict.

Talking seriously to Iran and Syria has been hard for the United States to do, but their implicit agreement must be reached for any partition to succeed. Weapons and fighters in the Iraq civil war have come from both countries. In any full-blown civil war, the Iranians would probably support the Iraqi Shi'a while Syria, Jordan, Egypt, and Saudi Arabia would likely support the Sunnis. Israel would probably support the Kurds.

Critics of partition have argued that the division of Iraq would allow the Shi'i Iranians to have too much influence in any southern autonomous region in Iraq. However, this might be an improvement over the current situation, because Iran now has great influence over the Shi'i-dominated central government, which has at least nominal control over all of Iraq—not just the Shi'i south. Furthermore, the Arab Shi'a running southern Iraq do not agree on many things with Iran's Shi'a, including their lack of support for a separation between religion and the state.[264] In fact, Shi'i Islam's holiest shrines are in Iraq, giving the Iraqi mullahs more stature than their Iranian counterparts. In short, Iranian dominance of any Shi'i autonomous region in southern Iraq is not preordained.

The Turks have threatened a full-blown invasion of northern Iraq to prevent Iraqi Kurdistan from being used as a haven for Kurdish rebels in Turkey. Yet, as noted earlier, despite Turkey's bluster and cross-border raids, for a decade and a half the Turks have tolerated an autonomous Kurdish region in northern Iraq. Substantial Turkish investments in Iraqi Kurdistan, the Turkish desire to get into the European Union, and Turkey's membership in NATO should make that nation more receptive to U.S. pressure to avoid such a tragic outcome. Furthermore, Turkish

inclusion in any partition talks and the veneer of a loose Iraqi confederation—rather than the creation of multiple independent Iraqi successor
states—might give Turkey a way to avoid invading and destabilizing
Iraqi Kurdistan.

13. Regions May Each Have a Different Form of Government

One allegation, made by critics of partitions, is that such division
creates a disproportionate share of undemocratic governments. Yet Jaroslav Tir's quantitative statistical analysis shows that partitions do not
create overwhelmingly undemocratic countries.[265]

In Iraq, although no reason exists as to why all component parts
might not eventually become liberal democracies, that ideal outcome
will probably not happen soon. After multiple wars and fifteen years
of the most grinding international economic sanctions, some of Iraq's
components simply may no longer be prosperous enough to sustain a
viable liberal democracy. Liberal democracy is more sustainable when
an emerging, relatively wealthy middle class begins to create the prerequisite political culture, which bubbles up from the bottom rather than
being imposed from the top by an outside power. That more open political culture may have developed among the prospering Kurds, but not yet
among the Sunnis and Shi'a.

The good news is that in any confederation, unlike in a more centralized federation or unified government, the component parts can have
different forms of regional governments. For example, the Kurds could
have liberal democracy, the Sunnis might opt for a secular dictatorship,
and the Shi'a might want a regime based on Islamic law. Although this
outcome may deviate from the original Bush administration goal of creating a unified, democratic Iraq, that goal was a pipe dream from the
beginning. The United States now needs to accept reality in order to
have any chance of getting out of a hopeless situation that is costing
much U.S. blood and treasure.

14. An International Peacekeeping Force May Be Needed for a Time After Partition

Although "peacemaking" by great powers or the international community is rarely successful, if all Iraqi groups could arrive at an agreement to partition the country, an international force—used for the limited "peacekeeping" mission of temporarily keeping the various Iraqi militias apart—might have a chance of succeeding. A force with such a limited mission was successful in keeping Israeli and Egyptian forces separated in the Sinai desert after a cessation of hostilities had already taken hold. International forces merely ensured that the two rival forces stayed out of contact, thereby decreasing the chances that an armed incident could escalate into a war.

Similarly, an international force could patrol the borders between Iraq's autonomous regions to keep ethno-sectarian militias policing their own territories apart so they wouldn't come into contact with each other. In contrast to the long-term existence of the Sinai force, however, an international contingent in Iraq should have a mandate of limited duration. Also, an international force in Iraq should have no residual troops from the hated U.S. occupier. As noted earlier, in any partition, a complete U.S. troop withdrawal should be used to compel the Shi'i- and Kurd-dominated Iraqi government to negotiate in good faith over the sharing of oil fields with the Sunnis. If the various Iraqi groups all agreed on partition, the nations of the international community might be much more willing to contribute troops for peacekeeping in Iraq than they have been to send forces to facilitate continued U.S. occupation of that country.

15. Caution: Autonomous Regions May Eventually Turn into Independent States

In some cases, ethno-sectarian groups gaining autonomy regard this status merely as a temporary way station toward independence. In a previously mentioned case, Mongolia achieved autonomy from China but really wanted, and later gained, independence. Similarly, after the 1999 war, Kosovo became an autonomous province of Serbia under the protection of the United Nations, but it was clear even then that Albanian Kosovars wanted an independent state. During the breakup of the Soviet Union, Mikhail Gorbachev unsuccessfully tried to salvage some sort of union by proposing a loose confederation of "sovereign" republics that would still give the Soviet central government control over defense, foreign policy, finance, gold, diamonds, and other strategic reserves.[266] But the republics would have none of it and became independent states. Thus history shows that sometimes it is hard to put the brakes on ethnosectarian desires for complete independence.

In Iraq, ultimately the Kurds would like their own state, and autonomy under a loose Iraqi confederation is likely only a temporary stop on the way to that goal. But in the short to medium term, Kurdistan being under an Iraqi confederation may take some of the pressure off the Turkish government to invade the Kurdish sector of Iraq. This is an important incentive for the Iraqi Kurds not to seek immediate independence. As the years pass, Turkey hopefully will get used to an autonomous Kurdistan—it has already been forced to do so for some time.

The Shi'a may also pursue the "autonomy to eventual independence" route. If they do, the Sunnis will be forced to do the same. But the ultimate breakup of Iraq should not be feared if it's done slowly and peacefully.

5

Conclusion

DESPITE THE U.S. GOVERNMENT'S AVOIDANCE of partition as an overt solution for the instability in Iraq, its actions on the ground reinforce regional autonomy in the country and the likelihood of such an eventual outcome. Yet for the long term, the current unrecognized, unratified, and incomplete partition risks a full-blown ethno-sectarian civil war.

Critics of partitioning Iraq have used historical examples—principally the partitions of Ireland in 1921, the Indian subcontinent in 1947, and Palestine in 1948—to attempt to discredit this solution. They allege that partition will increase violence and instability and lead to undemocratic outcomes. Yet even these violent partitions may have saved lives in the long term by at least partially separating the warring factions. In any event, the long-term violence was not caused by the partitions themselves, but by the fact that the partitions were incomplete. Moreover, the critics ignore many less celebrated successful, and even peaceful, partitions.

Iraq already has a de facto partition, with local militias providing security and other services in the Kurdish north and in areas in the central and southern regions of the country. Although not formally recognizing this reality, Bush administration policy implicitly accepted it by shifting to work with local militias rather than fighting them. The Obama administration has continued this policy. However, this unrecognized and unratified partition is dangerous. Because the U.S. troop surge has failed to remedy the underlying factors causing the sectarian and other violence in Iraq—the underlying cleavages in Iraqi society—the carnage will likely increase again after the surge is long over. The United States must use the threat of a quick U.S. troop withdrawal to give Iraq's ethno-sectarian groups a powerful incentive to negotiate a partition of the country into a loose confederation of autonomous regions or even three or more independent states. Iraq will likely eventually be partitioned—either peacefully with an agreed-upon "soft" division or a bloody full-blown civil war. Drawing lessons from historical partitions, this book attempts to give suggestions on the dos and don'ts for implementing a successful soft partition of Iraq.

Such dismemberment of Iraq may not be what the Bush or Obama administrations would have liked, but the illusion that Iraq can be a peaceful unified democratic state has to be dropped before such pie-in-the-sky dreams lead to an all-out bloodbath. The situation in Iraq is still dicey enough that unified, democratic fantasies have to be abandoned.

A large bipartisan majority in the U.S. Senate faced this reality and, in a step in the right direction, voted 75 to 23 for a nonbinding resolution in favor of decentralizing Iraq.[267] Predictably, the U.S. and Iraqi governments continued to oppose this concept. For decentralization to work, these two players and, most important, all ethno-sectarian groups in Iraq must ratify and adjust the de facto partition already in existence.

Despite the reduction in violence from essentially buying off Sunni and Shi'i Mahdi groups, this progress will likely erode if, as is likely, no political reconciliation can be achieved in this fractured land. The rival militias are likely biding their time until U.S. forces leave—all now having been armed by that same foreign occupier.

The de facto partition of Iraq needs to be recognized, ratified by an agreement among all ethno-sectarian groups, and made "virtually complete" by adjusting borders and the voluntary movement of peoples. Getting a political agreement among Iraqi groups—which would establish borders that take into account resources (such as oil) and cultural and religious sites and does not strand substantial minorities on the wrong side of the line—will be challenging. The failure to do so, however, will unfortunately likely result in a full-blown Iraqi civil war. In other words, the partition of Iraq will probably happen one way or another. A preventive, largely peaceful partition might avoid the bloody eventual division of Iraq.

Many leading Republicans and Democrats, including those in both the Bush and Obama administrations, favored keeping at least some U.S. troops in Iraq seemingly for perpetuity. The Obama administration has pledged to withdraw all "combat" troops from Iraq but apparently plans to leave large residual forces and simply avoid describing them as such.

Yet the Shi'i-Kurd government, being propped up by these forces, has no incentive to reconcile with the Sunnis. To give the Iraqis a powerful incentive to reach a partition agreement—especially a critical deal between the Kurds and Sunni Arabs to gerrymander the border of Kurdistan in order to give the Kurds control of more Kurdish-populated areas in exchange for the Sunnis getting more oil fields—the U.S. should announce that it will rapidly withdraw all forces from Iraq at a certain date. If that stark reality fails to persuade the Iraqis to reach a partition deal, the United States should rest assured that it has done all it could to stabilize Iraq, that a full-blown civil war is now inevitable, and that U.S. forces should not remain in the middle of it. In other words, the United States should then make good on the threat to withdraw all of its forces rapidly.

Notes

Chapter 1

1. Visser, Reider. 2008. "Historical Myths of a Divided Iraq." *Survival* 5 (2): 98–102.
2. Black, Edwin. 2004. *Banking on Baghdad: Inside Iraq's 7,000-Year History of War, Profit, and Conflict.* Hoboken, New Jersey: John Wiley and Sons, Inc., 53.
3. See Stansfield, Gareth. 2007. *Iraq: People, History, Politics.* Cambridge, U.K.: Polity Press, 18, 59–60. He notes correctly that the modern day Shi'i–Sunni cleavages are not based on sectarian differences alone, but also derive from Sunni political and economic dominance over the Shi'a during the Ottoman Empire and in every Iraqi government up until the U.S. deposed Saddam Hussein. In addition the Shi'i community is more religious in general compared to that of the Sunnis (today there are no secular Shi'i political parties).
4. Tripp, Charles. 2007. *A History of Iraq,* 3rd ed. Cambridge, U. K.: Cambridge University Press, 28.
5. Sluglett, Peter. 2007. "The Implications of Sectarianism in Iraq." *Journal of Middle Eastern Politics,* II (10): 49.
6. Black, *Banking on Baghdad,* 54–55, 68–69, 77, 79, 82, 83, 86–88.
7. Stansfield, *Iraq: People, History, Politics,* 31–32.
8. Hourani, Albert. 1991. *A History of the Arab Peoples.* New York: Warner Books, 448–449.
9. Stansfield, *Iraq: People, History, Politics,* 25.
10. Black, *Banking on Baghdad,* 170, 181–183, 187–190, 196–197, 241, and Hourani, *A History of the Arab Peoples,* 476.
11. Black, *Banking on Baghdad,* 196–197, 207–210.
12. Black, *Banking on Baghdad,* 213–214, 217–218, 242–243, 288–290, and Tripp, *A History of Iraq,* 58–59.
13. Stansfield, *Iraq: People, History, Politics,* 28. Stansfield took phrases in quotes from Charles Tripp in Gregory, Dick. 2004. *The Colonial Present.* Oxford: Blackwell Publishing, 145.
14. Tripp, *A History of Iraq,* 30–31.
15. Stansfield, *Iraq: People, History, Politics,* 28–29.
16. Oren, Michael B. 2007. *Power, Faith, and Fantasy: America in the Middle East 1776 to the Present.* New York: W.W. Norton & Company, 381.
17. Oren, *Power, Faith, and Fantasy,* 378.
18. Black, *Banking on Baghdad,* 174, 176, 226–227, and Hourani, *A History of the Arab Peoples,* 476.
19. Stansfield, *Iraq: People, History, Politics,* 63, 66–67.
20. Sluglett, "Implications of Sectarianism," 50.
21. Tripp, *A History of Iraq,* 45.
22. Stansfield, *Iraq: People, History, Politics,* 43, 82.
23. Stansfield, *Iraq: People, History, Politics,* 82, 103.

24. Tripp, *A History of Iraq*, 48.
25. Black, *Banking on Baghdad*, 214–217, 243–244, 247, 253–262, 269–270, 273, 281, 285, 293.
26. Tripp, *A History of Iraq*, 73–74.
27. Tripp, *A History of Iraq*, 93.
28. Oren, *Power, Faith, and Fantasy*, 442.
29. Black, *Banking on Baghdad*, 319–329.
30. Black, *Banking on Baghdad*, 353.
31. Stansfield, *Iraq: People, History, Politics*, 5–6, 194–196, 198.
32. Black, *Banking on Baghdad*, 355, 356, 358–362, and Hourani, *A History of the Arab Peoples*, 409.
33. Black, *Banking on Baghdad*, 362–363, and Hourani, *A History of the Arab Peoples*, 434.
34. Tripp, *A History of Iraq*, 162–164.
35. Hourani, *A History of the Arab Peoples*, 404–405, and Black, *Banking on Baghdad*, 363.
36. Tripp, *A History of Iraq*, xiii, 171.
37. Tripp, *A History of Iraq*, 199–200.
38. Oren, *Power, Faith, and Fantasy*, 59, 536.
39. Hourani, *A History of the Arab Peoples*, 417, and Black, *Banking on Baghdad*, 365–367.
40. Tripp, *A History of Iraq*, 320.
41. Tripp, *A History of Iraq*, 217.
42. Tripp, *A History of Iraq*, 218.
43. Hourani, *A History of the Arab Peoples*, 432.
44. Black, *Banking on Baghdad*, 368–369, and Oren, *Power, Faith, and Fantasy*, 560.
45. Tripp, *A History of Iraq*, 230–231.
46. Hourani, *A History of the Arab Peoples*, 434.
47. Tripp, *A History of Iraq*, 238.
48. Oren, *Power, Faith, and Fantasy*, 564.
49. Tripp, *A History of Iraq*, 248.
50. Oren, *Power, Faith, and Fantasy*, 568.
51. Tripp, *A History of Iraq*, 254–258.
52. Polk, William R. 2007. *Violent Politics: A History of Insurgency, Terrorism, and Guerrilla War, From the American Revolution to Iraq*. New York: HarperCollins, 206.
53. Tripp, *A History of Iraq*, xiii, xiv, 42–43, 54–55, 60–62, 65–66, 70–71, 72, 77, 79–82, 84–86, 110, 138, 151–152, 195, 203, 208–209.
54. Tripp, *A History of Iraq*, 4–5.
55. Tripp, *A History of Iraq*, 300–301.
56. Stansfield, *Iraq: People, History, Politics*, 168, 192–193, 198.

Chapter 2

57. Polk, *Violent Politics*, xvii.
58. O'Hanlon. Michael, 2003. "Shinseki vs. Wolfowitz," *Washington Times*, March 4, 2003. http://www.brookings.edu/views/op-ed/ohanlon/20030304.htm.
59. Knight-Ridder. 2003. "Few Iraqis See Americans as Liberators, Survey Finds." October 24, 2003.
60. Quoted in Al-Khabbaz, Yusuf. 2004. "Lessons from Japan for the U.S. Occupation of Iraq," Media Monitors Network, September 2, 2004. http://usa.mediamonitors.net/content/view/full/9342/.
61. Kurth, James. 2004. "Iraq: Losing the American Way." *American Conservative*, March 15, 2004. http://www.amconmag.com/2004_03_15/print/featureprint.html.
62. Basham, Patrick. 2004. "Can Iraq Be Democratic?" *Cato Institute Policy Analysis* (505), 13.
63. "Can Iraq Be Democratic?" 16.

64. Kagan, Robert. 2004. "Lowering Our Sights." *Washington Post*, May 2, 2004, B07.

65. Hersh, Seymour. 2004. "Plan B." *New Yorker*, June 28, 2004.

66. Shah, Anup. 2003. "United Nations Reports on Massive Death Toll From Sanctions." *Global Issues* (May 22, 2003): 4. http://www.globalissues.org/Geopolitics/Middle East/Iraq/Sanctions.asp#UnitedNationsreportsonmassivedeathtoll- fromsanctions.

67. Watkins, Susan. 2004. "Vichy on the Tigris." *New Left Review* 28 (July–August, 2004), 8.

68. Editorial, *New York Times*, August 9, 2004, A18; and Lins de Albuquerque, O'Hanlon, and Unikewicz, "The State of Iraq."

69. CNN. 2004. "McCain: Bush Not Straight Enough on Iraq: Senators of Both Parties Criticize His Picture of Conditions There." CNN.com, September 19, 2004. http://www.cnn.com/2004/ALLPOLITICS/09/19/iraq.senators; Hagel quoted in Landay, Jonathan. 2004. "GOP Senators Rebuke Bush for Plan to Diverting Iraq Funds." Knight-Ridder, September 16, 2004. http://www.commondreams.org/headlines04/0916–03.htm; and Slavin, Barbara. 2004. "Senators Slam Administration on Iraq." *USA Today*, September 15, 2004. http://www.usatoday.com/news/washington/2004–09–15-sens-iraq_x.htm.

70. Quoted in Kroft, Steve. 2004. "Gen. Zinni: 'They've Screwed Up,'" May 21, 2004. http://www.cbsnews.com/stories/2004/05/21/60minutes/main618896.shtml. Gen. Zinni was interviewed by the CBS program *60 Minutes*.

71. Hoar and Swannack quoted in McManus, Doyle. 2004. "Iraq Setbacks Change Mood in Washington: Lawmakers in Both Parties As Well As Some Military Leaders Fear the Occupation Is Heading for Failure. Bush Stands Firm, But U.S. Goals May Be Scaled Back." *Los Angeles Times*, May 23, 2004. http://www.commondreams.org/headlines04/0523–08.htm.

72. Quoted in Blumenthal, Sidney. 2004. "A Ruinous Trap of Their Own Making: Iraq Is Now More Dangerous to the U.S. Than When They Went to War." *The Guardian* (August 26) http://www.guardian.co.uk/comment/story/0,3604,1290870,00.html. The article consists of Blumenthal's interview with Larry Diamond.

73. Blumenthal, "A Ruinous Trap of Their Own Making."

74. Brzezinski, Zbigniew. "Face Reality: Lowered Vision." *The New Republic*, June 7 and 14: 16.

75. Anonymous [Michael Scheuer]. 2004. *Imperial Hubris: Why the West Is Losing the War on Terror*. Dulles, VA: Brassey's, 6–7. When the book was written, the author was an active senior U.S. intelligence official with nearly two decades of experience in covering militant Islam, Islamic insurgencies, terrorism, and South Asia, especially Pakistan and Afghanistan.

76. 9/11 Commission. 2004. *The 9/11 Commission Report: Final Report of the National Commission on Terrorist Attacks upon the United States*. New York: W. W. Norton, 66.

77. Pope, Hugh, and Bill Spindle. 2004. "Kurds' Success Makes It Harder to Unify All Iraq." *Wall Street Journal*, May 19, 2004, A1.

78. Tripp, *A History of Iraq*, 309–310.

79. Tripp, *A History of Iraq*, 1.

80. Galbraith, Peter. 2004. "How to Get Out of Iraq." *New York Review of Books* 51 (8). http://www.nybooks.com/articles/17103.

81. Chatham House. 2004. *Iraq in Transition: Vortex or Catalyst?* London: Chatham House, 2, 5.

82. Galbraith. 2004. "How To Get Out of Iraq."

83. Elazar, Daniel J. 1993. "International and Comparative Federalism." *Political Science and Politics* 26 (2): 190; and Riker, William. 1964. *Federalism: Origin, Operation, Significance*. Boston: Little, Brown, 5.

84. Saunders, Cheryl. 1995. "Constitutional Arrangements of Federal Systems." *Publius* 25 (2): 61.

85. Taylor, Paul. 1981. "The European Communities and the Obligations of Membership: Claims and Counterclaims." *International Affairs* 57 (2): 237–38.

86. Verney, Douglas V. 1995. "Federalism, Federative Systems, and Federations: The United States, Canada, and India." *Publius* 25 (2): 81.

87. Pinder, John. 1993. "The New European Federalism: The Idea and the Achievements." In *Comparative Federalism and Federation: Competing Traditions and Future Directions*. Ed. Michael

Burgess and Alain G. Gagnon. Toronto: University of Toronto Press, 45.

88. Hughes, Christopher. 1993. "Cantonalism: Federation and Confederacy in the Golden Epoch of Switzerland." In *Comparative Federalism and Federation*. Ed. Burgess and Gagnon, 155.

89. Peters, Ralph. 2003. "Break Up Iraq Now!" *New York Post*, July 10, 2003.

90. Newton, Hugh, and Morgan Norval. 2003. "Cracking the Sunni Triangle: It Makes Sense to Partition Iraq." *Washington Times*, August 11, 2003.

91. Davis, Eric. 2003. *Memories of State: Politics, History, and Collective Identity in Iraq*. Berkeley: University of California Press, 25, 28, 33. Davis provides a concise summary of this view but does not agree with it.

92. Davis, *Memories of State*, 11, 14, 17, 37.

93. Cox, Robert Henry and Erich Frankland. 1995. "The Federal State and the Breakup of Czechoslovakia." *Publius*, 25(1): 71.

94. Jehl, Douglas. 2004. "U.S. Intelligence Shows Pessimism on Iraq's Future: An Assessment for Bush: Civil War Called Possible—Tone Differs from Public Statements." *New York Times*, September 16, 2004, A1.

95. Ignatius, David. 2004. "Reassembling Iraq." *Washington Post*, May 14, 2004, A25.

96. Chatham House, *Iraq in Transition*, 9.

97. Saunders, "Constitutional Arrangements of Federal Systems," 61.

98. Elazar, "International and Comparative Federalism," 193, and Basham, "Can Iraq Be Democratic?" 1.

99. Milne, David. 2003. "One State or Two? Political Realism on the Cyprus Question." *The Round Table* 268: 155.

100. Dodd, Clement. 1999. "Confederation, Federation, and Sovereignty." *Perceptions: A Journal of International Affairs*, 4 (3). Can be found at http://www.kibris.gen.tr/english/articles/articles12.html.

101. Elazar, "International and Comparative Federalism," 194.

102. Elazar, Daniel J. 1998. *Constitutionalizing Globalization: The Postmodern Revival of Arrangements*. Lanham, MD: Rowman and Littlefield, 21.

103. Chatham House, *Iraq in Transition*, 6.

104. Brzezinski, "Face Reality," 17.

105. Energy Information Administration. "Country Analysis Briefs." http://www.eia.doe.gov/emeu/cabs/.

106. U.S. Department of State. "Background Notes." http://www.state.gov/www/background_notes/qatar_9711_bgn.html.

107. Author's calculations are as follows: 3.527696 billion barrels of crude oil imported into the United States in 2003 (Energy Information Administration. 2003. *Petroleum Supply Annual* 1. Washington, DC: U.S. Department of Energy, table 20, 53) multiplied by the $25.86 average price per barrel of oil in 2003 (Energy Information Administration. 2003. *Petroleum Marketing Annual*. Washington, D.C.: U.S. Department of Energy, table 1, 2) divided by $1.259705 trillion of total U.S. imports during 2003 (International Trade Administration. *U.S. Total Imports from Individual Countries, 1997–2003*. Washington, D.C.: U.S. Department of Commerce, table 7).

108. Cited in Taylor, Jerry. 1998. "Oil Not Worth the Fight." *Journal of Commerce*, 4A.

109. Losman, Donald. 2001. "Economic Security: A National Security Folly?" *Cato Institute Policy Analysis* 409, 7–8.

110. U.S. General Accounting Office. 2008. *Strategic Minerals: Extent of U.S. Reliance on South Africa* GAO/NSIAD-88-201. Washington, D.C.: U.S. General Accounting Office, June 1988, 3, 12, 25–27. The author helped write this report.

111. Losman, "Economic Security," 7–8.

112. Energy Information Administration. 2004. "Persian Gulf Oil and Gas Exports Fact Sheet." Washington, D.C.: U.S. Department of Energy.; and Eland, Ivan. 2001. *Putting "Defense" Back into U.S. Defense Policy: Rethinking U.S. Security in the Post-Cold War World*. Westport, CT: Praeger, 31.

113. Losman, "Economic Security," 7–8.

Chapter 3

114. Rubin, Michael. 2004. "Trust the Iraqis: Silent Majority." *The New Republic,* June 7 and 14, 24–25.

115. Basic Law. "Confederations and Federations." http://www.basiclaw.net/Principles/Confederations%20and%20Federations.htm.

116. Saunders, "Constitutional Arrangements of Federal Systems," 61.

117. Pinder, "The New European Federalism," 56, 64.

118. Verney, "Federalism, Federative Systems, and Federations.," 81; and Schmitt, Nicolas. 1994. "The Foreign Policy of Spanish Autonomous Communities Compared to That of Swiss Cantons." In *Evaluating Federal Systems.* Ed. Bertus de Villiers. Dordrecht, South Africa: Juta, 363–64.

119. Verney, "Federalism, Federative Systems, and Federations," 81; Saunders, "Constitutional Arrangements of Federal Systems," 61(19); and Schmitt, "The Foreign Policy of Spanish Autonomous Communities," 374.

120. Hughes, "Cantonalism," 167.

121. Elazar, *Constitutionalizing Globalization*, 3–4.

122. "Confederations and Federations." *Basic Law*, www.basiclaw.net/Principles/Confederations%20and%20Federations.htm.

123. Elazar, *Constitutionalizing Globalization*, 28.

124. Elazar, Daniel J. 1995. "From Statism to Federalism: A Paradigm Shift." *Publius* 25 (2): 5.

125. O'Dowd, Liam. 2002. Review of Chris Rumford's "The European Union: A Political Sociology." *Social Forces* 82 (4): 1645.

126. Taylor, "The European Communities," 241, 244, 250, 251.

127. Taylor, "The European Communities," 252.

128. Saunders, "Constitutional Arrangements of Federal Systems."

129. Pinder, "The New European Federalism," 58, 60, 62.

130. *The Economist*. "Towards an Uncertain Future." November 22, 2003.

131. Galbraith, "How to Get Out of Iraq," http://www.nybooks.com/articles/17103; and Gelb, Leslie. 2004. "What Comes Next?" *Wall Street Journal*, May 20, 2004, A12.

132. Krugman, Paul. 2004. "The Last Deception," *New York Times*, September 21, 2004, A35.

133. Centre d'Accueil, Genève Internationale. 1993. "The Swiss Political System." http://www.cagi.ch/en/systeme.htm; and Hughes, "Cantonalism," 164.

134. Elazar, "From Statism to Federalism," 5; and Elazar, *Constitutionalizing Globalization*, 10.

135. *The Economist*, "Towards an Uncertain Future."

136. Elazar, *Constitutionalizing Globalization*, 202.

137. Duchacek, Ivo. 1991. "Comparative Federalism: An Agenda for Additional Research," and Ostrom, Vincent. "A Computational-Conceptual Logic for Federal Systems of Governance." In *Constitutional Design and Power-Sharing in the Post-modern Epoch*. Ed. Daniel J. Elazar. Lanham, MD: Jerusalem Center for Public Affairs and University Press of America, 3–40.

138. Basham, "Can Iraq Be Democratic?," 4.

139. Cited in Miller, Greg. 2003. "Democratic Domino Theory 'Not Credible.'" *Los Angeles Times*, March 14, 2003, A1.

140. Basham, "Can Iraq Be Democratic?" 7–8, 10.

141. Cited in Elazar, "From Statism to Federalism" 5.

142. Chatham House, *Iraq in Transition*, 3.

143. Dodd, "Confederation, Federation, and Sovereignty," http://www.kibris.gen.tr/english/articles12/html.

144. Buchanan, James M. 1995. "Federalism as an Ideal Political Order and an Objective for Constitutional Reform." *Publius* 25 (2): 19.

145. Kurth, "Iraq: Losing the American Way," http://www.amconmag.com/2004_03_15/print/featureprint.html.

146. Rothbard, Murray. 2000. "Yugoslavian Breakup." In *The Irrepressible Rothbard: Essays of Mur-*

ray N. Rothbard. Ed. Llewellyn H. Rockwell Jr. Burlingame, CA: Center for Libertarian Studies. http://www.lewrockwell.com/rothbard/ir/Ch36.html.

147. Elazar, *Constitutionalizing Globalization*, 208, 216.

148. Pinkerton, James. 2004. "After Fallujah: Best Bet: Divide Iraq into Three States." *Newsday*, April 2, 2004. Can be found at http://www.newamerica.net/index.cfm?pg=article&DocID=1535.

149. Galbraith, "How to Get Out of Iraq," http://www.nybooks.com/articles/17103.

150. Pope and Spindle, "Kurds' Success," A1.

151. Yaphe, Judith. 2003. "Three States Is No Solution." Institute for National Strategic Studies, Nov. 25, 2003. Can be found at http://www.menavista.com/articles/yaphe.htm.

152. Gelb, "What Comes Next?" A12.

153. Chatham House, *Iraq in Transition*, 24.

154. Chatham House, *Iraq in Transition*, 4, 24.

155. Chatham House, *Iraq in Transition*, 24.

156. Chhor, Khathy. 2004. "Western Press Review: Partitioning Iraq, The Rise of Iran's Revolutionary Guards, NATO in Afghanistan." Radio Free Europe/Radio Liberty. http://www.rferl.org/featuresarticle/2004/05/73e1e4a8-a700-480f-96c6-ea860715fdeb.html.

157. Chatham House, *Iraq in Transition*, 8.

158. Luttwak, Edward. 2004. "Time to Quit Iraq (Sort Of)." *New York Times,* August 18, 2004, A21; and Chatham House, *Iraq in Transition*, 13.

159. For more on this viewpoint, see Waterman, Stanley. 1996. "Partition, Secession and Peace in Our Time." *GeoJournal* 39 (4): 345–352.

160. Kaufmann, Chaim D. 1998. "When All Else Fails: Ethnic Population Transfers and Partitions in the Twentieth Century." *International Security* 23 (2): 121, 123.

161. Sunstein, Cass R. 1991. "Constitutionalism and Secession." *The University of Chicago Law Review* 58 (2): 645–646.

162. Olcott, Martha Brill. 1991. "The Soviet (Dis)Union." *Foreign Policy* 82: 121–122.

163. Kaufmann, Chaim D. 1996. "Possible and Impossible Solutions to Ethnic Civil Wars." *International Security* 20 (4): 137.

164. Dorff, Robert H. 1994. "Federalism in Eastern Europe: Part of the Solution or Part of the Problem?" *Publius*, 24(2): 101.

165. Elazar, Daniel J. 1985. "Federalism and Consociational Regimes." *Publius* 15: 22.

166. Ra'anan, Uri, Maria Mesner, Keith Armes, and Kate Martin, eds. 1991. *State and Nation in Multi-Ethnic Societies: The Breakup of Multinational States*. New York: Manchester University Press.

167. Cohen, Gary B. 1993. Review of Ra'anan, Mesner, Armes, and Martin, eds. "State and Nation in Multi-Ethnic Societies," *Slavic Review*, 52: 148–149.

168. Dorff, "Federalism in Eastern Europe," 112.

169. Dorff, "Federalism in Eastern Europe," 100.

170. Gettleman, Jeffrey. 2007. "Ex-Rebels Quit Unity Government in Sudan." *New York Times*, October 12, 2007, A8.

171. Waterman, "Partition, Secession and Peace in Our Time," 348, 350, 351.

172. Etzioni, Amitai. 2007. "Plan Z for Iraq." *National Interest*. November/December, 44.

Chapter 4

173. Zakaria, Fareed. 2007. "Realism on the March." *Washington Post*, November 8, 2007, A27.

174. See Tir, Jaroslav. 2002. "Letting Secessionists Have Their Way: Can Partitions Help End and Prevent Ethnic Conflicts?" *International Interactions* 28, 275–276; and Waterman, "Partition, Secession and Peace in Our Time," 349, 350.

175. Cohen, Roger. 2007. "A Surreal State." *New York Times*, December 17, 2007, A29.

176. Kaufman, Stuart. 1997. "The Fragmentation and Consolidation of International Systems." *International Organization* 51 (2): 201–202.

177. Mosley, D. J. 1971. "Diplomacy and Disunion in Ancient Greece." *Phoenix* 25 (4): 324, 330; and Kaufman, "Fragmentation and Consolidation," 182, 190–191, 194, 195, 199.
178. Halecki, Oscar. 1945. "The Sixth Partition of Poland." *The Review of Politics* 7 (2): 143–144.
179. Rankin, George. 1940. "Legal Problems of Poland after 1918." *Transactions of the Grotius Society* 26: 1–3, 7.
180. Halecki, "The Sixth Partition of Poland," 144–145.
181. Young, Robert A. 1994. "How Do Peaceful Secessions Happen?" *Canadian Journal of Political Science*, 27:4 (Dec. 1994): 777, 786, 790.
182. Dorff, "Federalism in Eastern Europe," 103–104.
183. Harris, Chauncy D. 1993. "New European Countries and Their Minorities." *Geographical Review* 83 (3): 303–304, 306, 316.
184. Dorff, "Federalism in Eastern Europe," 108.
185. Sunstein, "Constitutionalism and Secession," 662.
186. Editor. 1907. "The Dissolution of the Union of Norway and Sweden." *The American Journal of International Law* 1 (2): 440–441.
187. Young, "How Do Peaceful Secessions Happen?" 777–778, 780, 781, 782; and Editor, "Dissolution of the Union of Norway and Sweden," 440–444.
188. Young, "How Do Peaceful Secessions Happen?" 778–780, 786, 789, 791.
189. Haile, Semere. 1987. "The Origins and Demise of the Ethiopia-Eritrea Federation." *A Journal of Opinion* 15: 9–17.
190. Connell, Dan. 1998. "From Alliance to the Brink of All-Out War: Explaining the Eritrea-Ethiopia Border Crisis." *Middle East Report* 208: 40–41.
191. Khan, Yasmin. 2007. *The Great Partition: The Making of India and Pakistan*. New Haven and London: Yale University Press, 105–106.
192. Khan, *The Great Partition*, 3–6, 97, 126.
193. Oren, *Power, Faith, and Fantasy*, 484–486, 488–489, 491–493, 498–502.
194. Rankin, "Legal Problems of Poland," 1–3, 7.
195. Khan, *The Great Partition*, 3–4, 87.
196. Etzioni, "Plan Z," 46.
197. Kessler, Glenn. 2008. "When the Data Don't Really Measure Up." *Washington Post*, April 9, 2008, A11.
198. Mill, John Stuart. 1958 [1861]. *Considerations on Representative Government*. New York: Liberal Arts Press, 230–233.
199. Tir, Jaroslav. 2005. "Keeping the Peace after Secession: Territorial Conflicts Between Rump and Secessionist States." *Journal of Conflict Resolution* 49 (5): 715, 721, 735–736.
200. Tir, "Letting Secessionists Have Their Way," 266.
201. Bookman, Milica Z. 1994. "War and Peace: The Divergent Breakups of Yugoslavia and Czechoslovakia." *Journal of Peace Research* 31 (2): 176; and Harris, "New European Countries," 313.
202. Sunstein, "Constitutionalism and Secession," 643.
203. Dorff, "Federalism in Eastern Europe," 108.
204. Sekelj, Laslo. 2000. "Parties and Elections: The Federal Republic of Yugoslavia-Change Without Transformation." *Europe-Asia Studies* 52 (1): 57.
205. Bookman, "War and Peace," 176–177, 183–184.
206. Kaufmann, "When All Else Fails," 126–132.
207. Pandey, Gyanendra. 1999. "Can a Muslim Be an Indian?" *Comparative Studies in Society and History* 41 (4): 614.
208. Khan, *The Great Partition*, 206, 208.
209. Khan, *The Great Partition*, 135.
210. Kaufmann, "When All Else Fails," 132–144.
211. Milne, R.S. 1996. "Singapore's Exit from Malaysia: The Consequences of Ambiguity." *Asian Survey* 6 (3): 175, 177, 178–179.
212. Chua, Amy. 2007. *Day of Empire: How Hyperpowers Rise to Global Dominance—and Why They Fall*. New York: Doubleday, 211, 226.

213. Oren, *Power, Faith, and Fantasy*, xx.

214. Khan, *The Great Partition*, 155.

215. Khan, *The Great Partition*, 97.

216. Sunstein, "Constitutionalism and Secession," 659.

217. Energy Information Administration, U.S. Department of Energy, "Country Analysis Briefs." http://www.eia.doe.gov/emeu/cabs/.

218. Chhor, "Western Press Review." http://www.rferl.org/featurearticle/2004/05 /73e1e4a8–9700–480f-9bcb-ea860715fdeb.html.

219. Galbraith, "How to Get Out of Iraq," http://www.nybooks.com/articles/17103.

220. Walt, Vivienne. 2007. "Iraqi Oil: More Plentiful than Thought." *Time.com*, April 24, 2007.

221. Gelb, Leslie. 2003. "Three-State Solution." *New York Times*, November 25, 2003. http://www. nytimes.com/2003/11/25/opinion/25GELB.html.

222. Mulama, Joyce. 2004. "Sudan: Another Step Towards Lasting Peace." *Inter Press Service* (Johannesburg), May 27, 2004, http://allafrica.com/stories/printable/200405270810.html.

223. Tir, "Letting Secessionists Have Their Way," 267–268.

224. Khan, *The Great Partition*, 97.

225. Editor. 2007. "Sovereignty and Limits for Kosovo," *New York Times*, October 5, 2007, A26.

226. Oren, *Power, Faith, and Fantasy*, 494–495.

227. Kaufmann, "When All Else Fails," 144–148, 155.

228. Watson, Geoffrey R. 2005. "The 'Wall' Decisions in Legal and Political Context." *The American Journal of International Law* 99 (1): 6–7, 26.

229. United Nations High Commission for Refugees. 1992. "Working Document for the Humanitarian Issues Working Group of the International Conference on the Former Yugoslavia." Geneva, Switzerland: UNHCR.

230. Khan, *The Great Partition*, 3–4, 155–156, 158.

231. For an example of these policy desires, see Mansfield, Anna Morawiec. 2003. "Ethnic but Equal: The Quest for a New Democratic Order in Bosnia and Herzegovina." *Columbia Law Review* 103 (8): 2,066, 2,089.

232. Bose, Sumantra. 2005. "The Bosnian State a Decade after Dayton." *International Peacekeeping* 12 (3): 331.

233. Kaufmann, "When All Else Fails," 125.

234. Khan, *The Great Partition*, 100, 102, 128, 131–132.

235. Mansfield, "Ethnic but Equal," 2,093.

236. Sunstein, "Constitutionalism and Secession," 644.

237. Bookman, "War and Peace," 183.

238. Carpenter, Ted Galen. 2007. "Escaping the Trap: Why the United States Must Leave Iraq." *Cato Institute Policy Analysis* 588: 13.

239. Bose, "The Bosnian State," 325–326.

240. Mansfield, "Ethnic but Equal," 2,061.

241. Kaufmann, "When All Else Fails," 120. For examples of other research in this growing body of literature, see also Christie, Clive J. 1992. "Partition, Separatism, and National Identity." *Political Quarterly* 63 (1): 68–78; Byman, David. 1997. "Divided They Stand: Lessons about Partition from Iraq and Lebanon." *Security Studies* 7 (1): 1–29; Weiner, Myron S. 1996. "Bad Neighbors, Bad Neighborhoods: An Inquiry into the Causes of Refugee Flows." *International Security* 21 (1): 37–38; Kaufmann, "Possible and Impossible Solutions to Ethnic Civil Wars," 136–175; and Posen, Barry R. 1993. "The Security Dilemma and Ethnic Conflict." In Ed. Michael E. Brown. *Ethnic Conflict and International Security*. Princeton, NJ: Princeton University Press, 103–124.

242. Mansfield, "Ethnic but Equal," 2,057–2,077; and Bose, "The Bosnian State," 326.

243. Remarks by Haris Silajdzic, a member of the three-person presidency of Bosnia and Herzegovina, at the Paul Nitze School of Advanced International Studies, Johns Hopkins University, November 9, 2007.

244. Cviic, Christopher. 1999. Review of Bildt, Carl. 1998. *Peace Journey: The Struggle for Peace in Bosnia*. London: Weidenfeld and Nicolson. In *International Affairs* 75 (2): 431.
245. Bose, "The Bosnian State," 324.
246. Bose, "The Bosnian State," 333.
247. Wisler, Dominique. 2007. "The International Civilian Police Mission to Bosnia and Herzegovina: From Democratization to Nation-Building." *Police Practice and Research* 8 (3): 254–255, 261–262, 265–267.
248. Bose, "The Bosnian State," 327, 329.
249. Bose, "The Bosnian State," 328.
250. Etzioni, "Plan Z," 45.
251. Etzioni, "Plan Z," 45.
252. Etzioni, "Plan Z," 46.
253. Bookman, "War and Peace," 180.
254. Etzioni, "Plan Z," 45.
255. Tir, "Peace after Secession," 721.
256. Tir, "Letting Secessionists Have Their Way," 261, 279–284, 285–286.
257. Milne, "Singapore's Exit from Malaysia," 181, 183.
258. Tir, "Peace after Secession," 736.
259. Tir, "Peace after Secession," 720.
260. Rajan, M.S. 1972. "Bangladesh and After." *Pacific Affairs*, 45:2 (summer 1972), 200.
261. Bookman, "War and Peace," 175.
262. Heraclides, A. 1997. "The Ending of Unending Conflicts: Separatist Wars." *Millennium* 26: 679–707.
263. Shanker, Thom. 2007. "Divided They Stand, but on Graves." *New York Times*, August 19, 2007, Week in Review, 1, 4.
264. Etzioni, "Plan Z," 47.
265. Tir, "Letting Secessionists Have Their Way," 261.
266. Olcott, "The Soviet (Dis)Union," 131–132.
267. Agence France Presse. 2007. "US Senate votes to support dividing Iraq on sectarian basis," September 26, 2007. http://afp.google.com/article/aleqm5hgjf7iu1btwerklwuhkbuu5gfwqw.

Index

About the Author

IVAN ELAND is Senior Fellow and Director of the Center on Peace & Liberty at the Independent Institute. Dr. Eland is a graduate of Iowa State University and received an M.B.A. in applied economics and a Ph.D. in Public Policy from George Washington University. He spent 15 years working for Congress on national security issues, including stints as an investigator for the House Foreign Affairs Committee and Principal Defense Analyst at the Congressional Budget Office. He also has served as Evaluator-in-Charge (national security and intelligence) for the U.S. General Accounting Office (now the Government Accountability Office), and has testified on the military and financial aspects of NATO expansion before the Senate Foreign Relations Committee, on CIA oversight before the House Government Reform Committee, and on the creation of the Department of Homeland Security before the Senate Judiciary Committee. Dr. Eland is the author of *Recarving Rushmore: Ranking the Presidents on Peace, Prosperity, and Liberty*; *The Empire Has No Clothes: U.S. Foreign Policy Exposed*; and *Putting "Defense" Back into U.S. Defense Policy*. He is a contributor to numerous volumes, including *Lessons from Iraq: The Next War*, and the author of 45 in-depth studies on national security issues.

His articles have appeared in *American Prospect, National Interest, Arms Control Today, Bulletin of the Atomic Scientists, Emory Law Journal, The Independent Review, Issues in Science and Technology, Mediterranean Quarterly, Middle East and International Review, Middle East Policy, Nexus, Chronicle of Higher Education, American Conservative, International Journal of World Peace*, and *Northwestern Journal of International Affairs*. Dr. Eland's popular writings have appeared in the *Los Angeles Times, Christian Science Monitor, San Francisco Chronicle, USA Today, Houston Chronicle, Dallas Morning News, New York Times, Chicago Sun-Times, San Diego Union-Tribune, Miami Herald, St. Louis Post-Dispatch, Newsday, Sacramento Bee, Orange County Register, Washington Times, Providence Journal, The Hill*, and *Defense News*. He has appeared on ABC's "World News Tonight," NPR, PBS, Fox News Channel, CNBC, Bloomberg TV, CNN, C-SPAN, MSNBC, Canadian Broadcasting Corp., Canadian TV, Radio Free Europe, Voice of America, BBC, Russia Today, al Jazeera, Press TV, and other TV and radio programs.

INDEPENDENT STUDIES IN POLITICAL ECONOMY

For further information and a catalog of publications, please contact:
THE INDEPENDENT INSTITUTE
100 Swan Way, Oakland, California 94621-1428, U.S.A.
510-632-1366 · Fax 510-568-6040 · info@independent.org · www.independent.org